LEARNING TO FLY - ESSENTIAL ELEMENTS

Connecting the Dots

John A Berkstresser

Copyright

Learning to Fly, Essential Element…Connecting the Dots
By John A. Berkstresser

Edited and Formatted by Lynne Berkstresser

Cover photograph by COL William J. "Shane" Keldahl, USAF Retired

Copyright © 2025 by John A Berkstresser

All rights reserved. No part of this book may be reproduced in any form or by any electronic or mechanical means, including information storage and retrieval systems, without written permission from the author, except for the use of brief quotations in a book review.

Printed in the United States of America

ISBN 979-8-218-53704-3

I dedicate this book to Anse Eugene "Windy" Windham who "Flew West" on August 17, 2014. Windy was my dear friend, mentor, and colleague, and without him this study would not exist.

* * *

* * *

Please consider sharing your thoughts and insights about Learning to Fly Essential Elements: Connecting The Dots with other aspiring pilots by leaving a review on Amazon. Just scan the QR code below. Thank You for Your Support!

Contents

Acknowledgments	vii
A Note on Aviation Terminology and Abbreviations	xi
INTRODUCTION: CONNECTING THE DOTS	1
1. FOUR STEPS TO BECOMING A STUDENT PILOT	5
2. THE PRIVATE PILOT CERTIFICATE	9
3. USING "THE CHECKLIST"	15
4. FLIGHT CONTROLS	21
5. FOUR FUNDAMENTALS OF FLIGHT	27
5.1 Straight and Level	28
5.2 Day-One Turn	30
5.3 Climb and Level Off + High Performance (HP)	37
5.4 Descents and Level Off: Enroute, Terminal, Final Approach + HP Procedures	42
6. THE GO-AROUND PROCEDURE	51
7. BASIC INSTRUMENTS (BI) TWO ELEMENTS: ROLL AND PITCH	55
8. SLOW FLIGHT AND SLIPS	65
8.1 Slow Flight	66
8.2 Sideslip	69
8.3 Forward Slip	72
9. STALLS	75
9.1 Approach to Landing Stall-Power Off	76
9.2 Takeoff/Departure Stalls-Power On	81
9.3 Accelerated Stall	83
10. STEEP TURNS	87
11. UNUSUAL (CRITICAL) ATTITUDES	93
12. TRACKING (CRAB)	97
13. GROUND REFERENCE MANEUVERS	101
13.1 Rectangular Course	102
13.2 S-Turns Across a Road	103
13.3 Turns About a Point	104

13.4 Eights Across a Road	105
13.5 Eights Along a Road	106
14. FOUR LEFT TURNING TENDENCIES	**109**
14.1 P-Factor	110
14.2 Spiraling Slipstream	111
14.3 Propeller Gyroscopic Precession	112
14.4 Torque Reaction	113
15. SPECIAL TAKEOFFS AND LANDINGS	**115**
15.1 Short Field Takeoff with Obstacle	116
15.2 Short Field Landing with Obstacle	118
15.3 Soft Field Takeoff	120
15.4 Soft Field Landing	121
16. AIRPORT OPERATIONS	**123**
16.1 The Anatomy of a Runway	125
16.2 The Three Airport Approach Gates	128
17. EMERGENCY OPERATIONS	**131**
17.1 Engine Failure - The Four S's	132
17.2 Confirmed Fire in the Air / Emergency Descent	133
17.3 Four Events Requiring Expedited Action	133
17.4 Declaring Minimum Fuel and Emergency Fuel	135
18. SRM: SINGLE PILOT/CREW RESOURCE MANAGEMENT	**139**
18.1 Pilot/Crew/Passenger Resource Management	140
18.2 Risk Management Models and Checklists	144
19. COMMUNICATIONS	**147**
19.1 Communicating with ATC and other Aircraft	148
19.2 Forty Must Know Pilot/ATC Radio Phrases for VFR Pilots	150
20. COMMON ABBREVIATIONS, SYMBOLS, AND ACRONYMS	**161**
20.1 Abbreviations and Symbols	161
20.2 Acronyms for Procedure and Safety Checklists	167
21. ADVANCED QUALIFICATION PROGRAM (AQP)	**171**
22. RECOMMENDED READING	**177**
Appendix: Aviation Terminology and Abbreviations	179
About the Author	181

Acknowledgments

*"Every person that comes into our life comes for a reason;
some come to learn and others come to teach."*
-- *Antoine de Saint-Exupéry*

Many people have influenced and encouraged me in my passion for flying throughout three-score years, and my devotion to aviation continues to thrive. Among many other extraordinary gifts, God granted me a love of airplanes and of those fortunate souls who feel the same way. In hindsight, I have no doubt that He also smoothed my path to enjoying an exciting and fulfilling life in aviation.

This book is the materialization of my flying experiences, both military and civilian, and the people associated with me. A byproduct of their influence, I would not be here if not for all of them.

Early on, I wanted to emulate my older brother, Blaine Berkstresser, who flew for the airlines and then became the chief pilot for Ashland Oil and Refining Company in Ashland, Kentucky. He, along with my uncle, Wallace Burkett, a WWII Air Force Pilot, were heroes to me, and I grew up wanting nothing more than to fly airplanes for a living.

Along the way my high school English teacher, Howard Walker, mentored me and influenced how I approached my chosen path. I would never have been a pilot if not for his wholehearted belief and ready encouragement.

I was privileged to fly with exceptional mentors during my military career: RADM E. E. "Ernie" Christensen, J. D. Davis, Scott Davis, and

Keith Mast to name just a few. Their leadership cemented my desire to continue with my aviation career, and I thank them. And when it came time to transition to civilian flying, fellow Naval Officer William Gordon and his wife, Nancy, befriended me by involving me in a flying club and, more importantly, making sure I never went hungry! I jest, but they became family, and I'm forever grateful to them.

Many others, too numerous to mention, gave positive direction and momentum to my life, but I must thank James F. McMartin, who helped me train for my airline profession. And Paul D. O'Connell for his help and mentoring leadership in my successful Captain upgrade as well as his strong support for this work. Thomas T. Burk assisted in editing the early manuscript of this book, and I humbly appreciate his input and confidence in my endeavor.

I deeply appreciate Dr. Dean D. Worthingstun's contribution to the content and organization of this work in the final months of its evolution. As an Air Force Academy graduate and subsequent Naval Flight Officer, his input was invaluable. Dean is now a hand surgeon and, not surprisingly, remains an avid aviator.

In the last few years of my instructing profession, COL William J. "Shane" Keldahl, USAF Retired, volunteered to join me in mentoring young, aspiring aviators. He could see that I was genuinely focused on teaching new pilot applicants, not building time. This book is not for time builders. Without COL Keldahl's encouragement and leadership, this project would never have come to fruition.

Special thanks also to CFII Josh Flowers, founder and owner of Aviation101 Productions, for his work in General Aviation (GA) through the Advanced Qualification Program (AQP) designed to address the GA fatal accident rate. His generous permission in allowing me to include his work in this book reflects his strong dedication and allows the pilot community as a whole to be a part of the solution. I continue to use his AQP material as part of my flight reviews, and I encourage other CFIs to review, understand, and provide an AQP approach to flight reviews. Our continued flying in GA depends upon it.

One of my most rewarding teaching successes is Peter O. Coltman, whom I began to mentor at age 14. He completed all of his ratings by age 18, his career ballooned, and he passed me up like I was standing still. He is the kind of pilot people write books about, and his resume reflects the story. Throughout the years Peter has remained a great positive influence for me, and I will always be grateful for his loyalty, friendship, and continued support.

My greatest debt; though, I reserve for Mr. Anse Eugene "Windy" Windham, who mentored me through my flight instructor ratings: CFI, CFII, and all the ground instructor ratings. Windy became associated with this present study in its infancy in 1980. The genesis of this work began as a little black book of 20 pages, conceived by Windy, to get me through my civilian flight instructor ratings.

He was not only instrumental in getting me through the instructor syllabus but also taught me how to effectively teach, supervising me through my first few student applicants. Many of the ideas in this book are his, and I am perpetually grateful to him for sharing his knowledge and expertise with me so many years ago.

Last but never least I thank my wife, Lynne Berkstresser, for tirelessly editing this book, making suggestions along the way, and contributing to its format and content design.

John A. Berkstresser

A Note on Aviation Terminology and Abbreviations

The Aviation Industry uses a host of abbreviations in its terminology, and retaining this information can be daunting to the novice pilot. Following common practice, in this text, the full Aviation Term will first be used along with its abbreviation in parentheses, e.g., Federal Aviation Administration (FAA). Subsequent entries of the term will be represented by only the abbreviation, e.g., FAA.

In an effort to simplify the reading of this text for the initiate, I have added an alphabetized appendix of the Aviation Terms used, along with their abbreviations. This additional information should greatly reduce the need to waste precious time searching back through the text for the pertinent Aviation Terms.

Introduction: Connecting The Dots

This book is for flight instructors, student pilots, and professional pilots alike. It is a learning/teaching tool to address years of failure to impart sound techniques, standardized procedures, and fundamental flying knowledge. It teaches fundamental flight training concepts and shows how to put them into practice. I call this *Connecting the Dots,* and it is the key signature of this training manual.

This focus on fundamentals contains the basic concepts required to fly an aircraft with confidence and explains how to practice flying in a manner that builds high knowledge and proficiency.

For every flight instructor reading this book, I present precisely what should be done on the training flight. The lessons provide standardized procedures for each task, followed by a detailed brief on why, how, and where we perform the task.

This formula is significant throughout the book because these fundamentals never change; they provide a clear foundation for all pilots that will stick with them regardless of what kind of flying they choose. All lessons and procedures herein lend themselves well to any flying syllabus or lesson plan.

LEARNING TO FLY - ESSENTIAL ELEMENTS

The Challenge of Developing an Individual into a Proficient Pilot Can Be Supported with a Set of Four Assumptions:

First, students learn to fly on the ground, not in the air. The aircraft is not an efficient classroom. The instructor must provide thorough introductory ground briefs before each flight to prepare the student—and reduce the stress—for what will be happening in the air.

Second, students learn not because of the flight instructor but in spite of the flight instructor. Given no other choice of instructors, a student will eventually figure out how to fly the machine. Depending on the quality of instruction, the student's flying ability may be fraught with bad habits and poor Aeronautical Decision Making (ADM) skills. A good flight instructor will precisely communicate what the student needs to know in the shortest time possible, always avoiding rhetorical questions, to allow the student to proficiently accomplish each task of the lesson.

Third, I find a lack of fundamental flight training being presented, or inappropriately presented, at the wrong place or time. Canvassing students' logbooks and finding a predominance of touch-and-go landings in the initial hours of their training, without an emphasis on their pre-solo maneuver requirements, is evidence of unbalanced instruction and may cause a false self-concept of proficiency. The initial hours of flight training must be spent honing their air work skills while learning and completing the required Federal Aviation Administration (FAA) pre-solo maneuvers.

Moreover, the Four Fundamentals of Flight (Straight and Level, Turns, Climbs, and Descents) may not be adequately addressed. Restating this premise, I would say one does not learn to fly in the traffic pattern (ex. touch and go maneuvers). All FAA pre-solo requirements must be taught to proficiency before you ever get to the traffic pattern, which is, by the way, an advanced ground reference maneuver.

Fourth, accomplish every procedure the same way every time. Flying is a cognitive activity. Regardless of technical stick-and-rudder

Introduction: Connecting The Dots

skills, a pilot flies with the brain. No matter how one utilizes the phases, levels, and laws of learning as described in the *Aviation Instructor's Handbook (FAA-H-8083-9B)*, I believe the ultimate goal with flight students is to teach them an **"Automatic Response Stage"** in their flying-skills development. In other words, a student/pilot must learn to complete procedures in the same way every time so that they "DO" without having to think.

This practice not only generates proficiency but also provides confidence in what students are doing. The buzzword for this is "Standardization." The military training commands, the airlines, and all business simulator training companies have it. I believe GA is getting better with standardization through the Airman Certification Standards (ACS) program; however, the high accident rate across the country indicates that we should do better—and we must.

For all those who have achieved the coveted wings of a pilot, we cannot forget what a privilege we have flying and navigating our complex skies. Yet, substantial numbers of fatal GA accidents are reported each month. It is significant and alarming that most of the accidents are avoidable. This cannot continue if we expect to keep enjoying this marvelous privilege.

Better training, with an emphasis on Fundamentals, would mitigate or erase these tragic events.

What I introduce in the following pages specifically addresses how to understand (cognitive) and apply (perform) the Four Fundamentals of Flight, *Connecting the Dots* in all regimes of flight. My main tools are procedures. Knowing what procedures to use, where to look, why you look, how to look, and when to look, provide a clear template on how to fly a plane.

* * *

Something to ponder until time for your Solo Flight: Leaving the earth on your own for the first time changes your life forever…

LEARNING TO FLY - ESSENTIAL ELEMENTS

Chapter 1
Four Steps to Becoming a Student Pilot

PREPARE FOR TAKEOFF!

1. Choose a Flight Instructor
2. Apply for a Student Pilot Certificate
3. Obtain Your Medical Certificate
4. Begin a Computer-Based Ground School

Choosing a Flight Instructor

A student builds the foundation to become a pilot by approaching flight training in the right way: choosing a flight instructor that meets his/her specific needs. This is a crucial first step for either a student pilot or an established pilot earning a new endorsement.

A Few Important Tips...

MEET WITH MORE THAN ONE...Remember, you are interviewing someone for a job, so try to meet with several instructors and compare them to one another. Contact flight schools, check online directories such as The National Association of Flight Instructors (NAFI) at Nafinet.org, and get recommendations from other students.

ASK QUESTIONS...Whether by phone or in person, don't shrink from asking questions. Ask about the instructor's background and credentials. What is his/her training philosophy? What steps does he/she use and how many hours will it take to get your Private Pilot Certificate? How does his/her schedule and availability align with yours? What are the costs involved? Billing and cancellation policies?

DO YOUR RESEARCH...Ask for references. The instructor should happily provide you with a list. Don't hesitate to contact the instructor's previous students. Find out how many of his/her students completed their training. Ask for *positive and negative* feedback.

SCHEDULE AN INTRODUCTORY FLIGHT LESSON...Once you have narrowed your list, ask to schedule a short, introductory lesson. Take this opportunity to gauge the instructor's teaching style and his/her commitment to helping you reach your goals.

ASK FOR AN OUTLINE...Ask the flight instructor to supply you with an outline of the requirements involved in getting your pilot certificate so that you know what is ahead. Remember, the flight instructor's primary duty is to equip student pilots with all the tools and information necessary to fly safely and competently.

Making Application for a Student Pilot Certificate

FAA Code of Federal Regulations (CFR) 61.83 states that to be eligible for a Student Pilot Certificate, the applicant must be able to speak, write, and understand the English language, and be at least age 16 (age 14 to pilot a glider or balloon). It's a good idea to complete this step as soon as possible. While you don't need a Student Pilot Certificate to take flying lessons, you *do* need one to fly solo. Proper planning is essential. Factors like weather, frequency of lessons, and financial status can influence the time it takes to solo. The average is around 15 hours, but I've had students needing as little as eight hours to solo, so one needs to be ready.

Four Steps to Becoming a Student Pilot

The student pilot can access and complete this application online using the Integrated Airman Certification and Rating Application (IACRA) website at IACRA.faa.gov.

If paper is preferred, use FAA form 8710-1 (faa-form-8710-1.pdffiller.com), and submit it to a Certified Flight Instructor (CFI), a Flight Standards District Office (FSDO), a FAA Designated Pilot Examiner (DPE), or an Airman Certification Representative (ACR) associated with a part 141 flight school.

The authorized individual will then process your application and submit the required documents to the FAA Airmen Certification Branch. The Student Pilot Certificate will be mailed to your address in approximately three weeks.

Be advised that utilizing the IACRA website will minimize the time it takes for this process to unfold. Ask your flight instructor to complete this application with you on the IACRA website.

There is no charge if the application is made directly to the FSDO; however, all other sources may charge a reasonable fee.

Obtaining a Medical Certificate

An authorized Aviation Medical Examiner (AME) will issue the medical certificate once the student pilot has passed a medical examination. There are three classes of Medical Certificates:

- First Class: for the Airline Transport Pilot (ATP)
- Second Class: for the Commercial Pilot
- Third Class: for the Student, Recreational, and Private Pilot

Your flight instructor should be able to provide you with the name of a local AME; however, a list of AMEs by area may be found at www.faa.gov/pilots/amelocator.

LEARNING TO FLY - ESSENTIAL ELEMENTS

Completing a Computer-Based Ground School

I recommend completing a Computer-Based Ground School Course before beginning your flight lessons. While students may complete ground-school training with their flight instructor or by attending in-person ground school classes run by flight schools, it is quicker, easier, and much less expensive to complete a computer-based training course. And the knowledge you gain from the course will enhance your learning experience as you begin your flight lessons. These courses are generally around 40 hours long, and your flight instructor will assist you in selecting one that is reputable.

Popular Computer-Based Ground School Courses

(These options are in alphabetical order and not by ranking.)

- Angle of Attack Online Ground School
- ASA Private Pilot Online Ground School
- Gleim Aviation Online Ground School
- Gold Seal Online Ground School
- King Schools
- Pilot Institute Online Ground School
- Rod Machado's 40-hour Private Pilot eLearning Ground School
- Sporty's Private Pilot Learn to Fly

Each of these online Ground-School Courses have unique and varied characteristics. Again, your instructor is an important resource and will be able to offer recommendations and help you sift through the details. Even so, I encourage you to also conduct your own research and choose one that most fits the specific goals you are trying to achieve.

Chapter 2
The Private Pilot Certificate

> The Private Pilot Certificate, often referred to as the Private Pilot License (PPL), is one of the most sought-after flying certificates to obtain because of its versatility.

Students don't need hundreds of flight hours to complete their training. This certificate allows pilots to fly virtually any aircraft, operate in Visual Flight Rules (VFR) Conditions, and build up additional ratings like instrument, commercial, multiengine, and flight instructor.

To become a private pilot, the student must ultimately pass the FAA Knowledge Test and the FAA Practical Test. Once the student has passed these tests, he/she will be issued the Private Pilot Certificate, which allows the holder to fly for private purposes only.

The following checklists with requirements taken from Federal Aviation Regulations (FAR) 61.103 provide general outlines of what to expect when exploring your flight training goals and possibilities. Be sure to ask a lot of questions in your research and arm yourself with the relevant information you need to make the best decisions for your particular situation.

LEARNING TO FLY - ESSENTIAL ELEMENTS

Become a Private Pilot Checklist

- Decide whether to pursue the Sport, Recreational, or Private Certificate.
- Meet the full eligibility requirements.
- Find a flight instructor or enter a pilot-training program.
- Take an introductory flight lesson.
- Schedule a FAA medical exam with a local AME (not required for Sport) to obtain a third-class medical certificate.
- Apply for a Student Pilot Certificate (your license to learn).
- Complete a ground school or home study course.
- Pass the FAA Knowledge Test.
- Complete flight training and earn the required endorsements.
- Pass the FAA Private Pilot Practical Test, which consists of an oral exam and a flight check.
- The Student Pilot Certificate will be replaced with a temporary Private Pilot Certificate. The FAA will issue a permanent certificate after reviewing your qualifications.
- Be age 17 to apply for and receive the Private Pilot Certificate

As previously stated in chapter one, the Student Pilot Certificate may be issued at age 16 (age 14 to fly gliders and balloons); however, **issuance of the Private Pilot Certificate requires that the student pilot be at least age 17** (age 16 to fly gliders and balloons).

The FAA Knowledge Test may be taken at age 15; however, you must present an authorization which proves you are ready to take the test. This authorization could be a certificate of graduation, a written statement, or a logbook endorsement. The test consists of 60 multiple-choice questions with three possible answers, the allotted time is two and a half hours, and the passing score is 70 percent. Retesting is possible with an instructor's endorsement, and it is valid for two years.

The FAA Private Pilot Practical Test comes after completing your pilot training, passing the FAA Knowledge Test, and getting your instructor's endorsements. The endorsements are proof that you have met all

The Private Pilot Certificate

the required practical-test standards and that you have demonstrated flight proficiency in a three-hour preparatory flight within two months of the test. It may be given by a FAA Inspector or a DPE and consists of an oral exam and a flight check, each lasting an average of one and a half hours.

Pre-Solo Requirements: Maneuvers and Procedures

Prior to the Solo flight, receive and log flight training for the following:

- Proper Flight Preparation Procedures, including Preflight Planning and Preparation, Powerplant (engine) Operation, and Aircraft Systems
- Taxiing or Surface Operations, including Runups
- Takeoffs and Landings, including Normal and Crosswind
- Straight and Level Flight, and Turns in both directions
- Climbs and Climbing Turns
- Airport Traffic Patterns, including Entry/Departure Procedures
- Collision Avoidance
- Windshear Avoidance
- Wake Turbulence Avoidance
- Descents, with and without Turns, using High and Low Drag Configurations
- Flight at Various Airspeeds from Cruise to Slow Flight
- Stall Entries from Various Flight Attitudes and Power Combinations with Recovery Initiated at the First Indication of a Stall and Recovery from a Full Stall
- Emergency Procedures
- Equipment Malfunctions
- Ground Reference Maneuvers
- Approaches to a Landing Area with Simulated Engine Malfunctions
- Slips to a Landing
- Go-Arounds

LEARNING TO FLY - ESSENTIAL ELEMENTS

The Solo Shirt Cutting Ceremony

This time-honored tradition dates back to the early days of aviation when, because of noisy conditions, flight instructors would tug on their students' shirts to inform them to make needed corrections. Nowadays, after the much-anticipated first solo flight, the instructor cuts out the back of the student's shirt to signify his/her new status as a solo pilot—no more tugging!

Many instructors traditionally make the cut in an upside down "V" to symbolize giving WINGS to the new aviator. The date and details of the solo flight, along with the instructor's signature, are written on the cutout portion, thus making it an important keepsake of a major milestone for the new pilot to remember forever.

Flight schools usually display a photo of the cutout on their walls as a tribute to the student's success and entry into the aviation community.

Private Pilot Requirements

This complete list also includes the Pre-Solo requirements:

- Preflight Operations: Pilot Qualifications, Airworthiness Requirements, Weather Information, Cross-Country Flight Planning, National Airspace System, Performance and Limitations, Operations of Systems, Human Factors, Checklist Usage, PAVE (ch. 18)
- Taxi, Before Takeoff Check, Communications and Light Gun Signals, Normal, Short Field and Soft Field Takeoffs and Landings, Climbs and Descents , Go-Arounds/Rejected Landings
- Forward Slips and Sideslips
- Slow Flight
- Steep Turns
- Unusual (Critical) Attitudes
- Power-On Stalls (Takeoff and Departure Stalls)
- Power-Off Stalls (Clean, Turning, Approach to Landing Stalls)

The Private Pilot Certificate

- Ground Reference Maneuvers
- Basic Instruments (Four Fundamentals of Flight), Radio Aids, Radar Vectors
- Cross-Country (Pilotage, Dead Reckoning, Radio Navigation, and Emergencies)
- Night Flight
- Emergency Operations, including Simulated Aircraft and Equipment Malfunctions

Aeronautical Experience for Aircraft Single-Engine Rating

Reference: FAR 61.109 Aeronautical Experience

40 Hours of Flight Time in a Single-Engine Aircraft Including

—20 Hours Flight Training from an Authorized Instructor:

- Three hours of Cross-Country flight training
- Three hours of Night Flight that includes one cross-country flight of over 100 nautical miles total distance and 10 takeoffs and landings to a full stop (with each landing involving a flight in the traffic pattern) at an airport
- Three hours of flight training on the Control and Maneuvering of an aircraft solely by reference to instruments, including straight and level flight, constant airspeed climbs and descents, turns to a heading, recovery from unusual flight attitudes, radio communications, and the use of navigation systems/facilities and radar services appropriate to instrument flight
- Three hours of flight training with an authorized instructor in preparation for the FAA Practical Test, which must have been performed within the preceding two calendar months from the month of the test
- Eight hours in Fundamental Flight Training with an instructor

LEARNING TO FLY - ESSENTIAL ELEMENTS

— 10 Hours of Solo Flight Time Consisting of At Least:

- Five hours of Solo Cross-Country time
- One Solo Cross-Country flight of 150 nautical miles total distance with full-stop landings at three points and one segment of the flight consisting of a straight-line distance of more than 50 nautical miles between takeoff and landing locations
- Three Takeoffs and Three Landings to a full stop (with each landing involving a flight in the traffic pattern) at an airport with an operating control tower

The average time to get a Private Pilot Certificate is 50 to 80 hours; although, time will vary with each individual depending on the local flight environment and the consistency of training.

Documents Requirements: Arrow PC

This acronym is a great memory aid to help pilots remember the documents which are legally required to be onboard an aircraft.

Airworthiness Certificate
Radio License (International flights only)
Registration (Aircraft)
Operating Limitations **(Pilot's Aircraft Operating Manual)**
Weight and Balance Data

Aircraft **P**lacards
Compass Card

Chapter 3
Using "The Checklist"

> The adherence of any "Checklist" is a necessary component of every aviation endeavor; they help pilots avoid complacency and missed steps to ensure safe and successful flights.

The Pilot In Command (PIC) must set a tone of skill and discipline with every flight. For example, when do you prepare for a good landing? It should begin days in advance by thinking about everything relevant to all aspects of preflight planning with the ensuing flight as well as with the post flight events. It's a good practice to develop a mental checklist which includes weather, Notice to Airmen (NOTAMS), and preliminary flight planning.

Once you're at the aircraft, its Pilot Operating Handbook (POH) provides a "Checklist" to cover all aspects of the safe inspection and operation of the aircraft. Its use is essential, regulatory and must be complied with at all times.

There seems to be a disconnect between GA's philosophy of checklist usage vs Part 135 (charter operations) and Part 121 (airline operations). Checklists should be designed and used to produce the most efficient

LEARNING TO FLY - ESSENTIAL ELEMENTS

and timely outcomes, always considering the safest end product. Training centers such as CAE, Flight Safety, and the airlines specifically define "The Checklists," which in turn determines how they are to be used.

Most GA schools and flight instructors do not delineate checklists in terms of definition and use. They seem to gravitate to the "See and Do" corner. The downside of this practice is the lack of understanding and proficiency when pilots are advanced to upper-level flying opportunities which require training in advanced simulators with all of their unique ways of completing checklists.

As I have previously mentioned, if you do everything the same way every time, advancing to the next step is so much easier. Why not use checklists with GA primary training the same way as in the advanced stages of training? This requires defining the types of checklists to determine which behavior is required. **Aircraft Checklists are Divided Into Four Groups:**

- NORMAL
- ABNORMAL
- EMERGENCY
- IMMEDIATE ACTION ITEMS

All four types of Checklists utilize a specific behavior.

Normal Checklists

In the professional world, **all Normal Checklists are preceded with a flow**. When a company or airline hires you, you are expected to memorize and execute the **flow** of each checklist without reading it from a list. The professionals mitigate undue time situations by utilizing Flow Checklists where they can, which saves a lot of time and money. How does that work? The greatest time waster is reading a checklist item, finding the switch, and moving the switch. It saves a lot of time to complete the **Switchology** (flow) by memory, then reading and

Using "The Checklist"

confirming The Checklist; you do not have to rush, and you do not sacrifice safety.

Why not teach **Flow Procedure** with GA primary flight training since students will eventually need to understand and perform the flow mindset as they advance to the professional aviation world. Many come unprepared and some do not make it through advanced training. I know one jet charter service that says, "If you do not have the Flow Checklist memorized, don't bother showing up at the simulator." This is the real world where time is money.

As I teach primary, I train my students to execute a "Flow." This is not a "See and Do." Once the flow is complete, the student reads the title of the current checklist being used and visually confirms while verbalizing each response while glancing at each switch. After the checklist responses are complete, the pilot now arrives at the most important part of the checklist: Calling it Complete.

Calling the Checklist Complete Will Close a Mental Loop

Example: After having just completed the "Before Start Checklist Flow," then reading all the items and responses out loud and confirming that each item was done, the student reads the title of the checklist and then calls it complete by stating: **"The Before Start Checklist is Complete."**

Remember, do not put the checklist you are holding in your hand down until you have announced it complete. Again, this closes a mental loop in a cognitive way, allowing you to know with 100-percent accuracy that all checklist items are checked and complete.

Every normal checklist during the flight, with few exceptions specifically addressed, should be accomplished this way. I begin my students' training this way from Day-One.

LEARNING TO FLY - ESSENTIAL ELEMENTS

Abnormal and Emergency Checklists

The **Abnormal and Emergency Checklists** are always completed as a **"See and Do."** The takeaway here is that you should never be in a hurry when commanding an aircraft at any time during its operation. Flows are not appropriate here, and this is very much enforced. **One should never rush any checklist, especially during a "See and Do."**

Reference my chapter on Four Events Requiring Immediate Action (sec. 17.3). These are the only exceptions I can think of where you need to be in a hurry in an aircraft. If there are more, they are very exceptional indeed.

Immediate Action Items Checklists

The last type of Checklist, **Immediate Action Items**, requires a completely memorized response; although, most of the airlines are doing away with this procedure. They utilize a Quick Reference Handbook especially designed to allow the non-flying pilot to address these problems in a timely fashion, mitigating any errors due to an inaccurate memory response.

However, many jet charter services still utilize an Immediate Action Items Checklist. Your training program will emphasize the requirement to work the procedure **by memory**. Fortunately, there are not many Immediate Action Items, but you need to be prepared. *Do not go to the simulator unprepared.*

We have covered the four checklist types which you will become intimately familiar with as you continue your flying life. The following pages in this book involve Procedures and Checklists. The Engine Failure Procedure (sec. 17.1), for example, is an immediate action items checklist for GA primary training, one of perhaps several authored by various aviation educators. I use this one in the book because of its relative ease as a memory aid. **Of course, your POH will always be your final guide.**

Using "The Checklist"

Other procedures listed in this book are explained in the following briefs associated with each particular procedure. These procedures are not checklists which you will find in your POH, but I include and explain them as a way for you to understand and perform the maneuvers required for your Private Pilot Checkride.

I hope you find them enlightening. The tidbits of information contained in each procedure and brief have proven invaluable, making my CFI teaching life very enjoyable and helping me to earn a Gold Seal Flight Instructor Rating. Enjoy learning and flying!

> When the time comes for the actual flight, Acronyms (ch. 20) have been designed to assist pilots in all aspects of preflight planning and can be very effective.

Chapter 4
Flight Controls

> Aircraft Flight Controls enable a pilot to control the direction and attitude of an aircraft in flight. Ground-School Prep will provide the necessary knowledge; meanwhile, here is a brief overview.

These basic mechanical systems date back to the earliest aircraft types and are still in use in the majority of light, GA aircraft. Cables, pulleys, rods, and chains transmit the movement of the flight deck controls to the appropriate control surfaces. More recent efforts to reduce weight for fuel savings have led designers of newer aircraft models to replace most of the mechanical components with computers and fiber optics. These newer control systems are called "Fly-By-Wire."

Flight controls are divided into two groups: Primary and Secondary. Primary flight controls are used to safely control an aircraft during flight and consist of ailerons, elevators (or, in some installations, stabilators), and rudder. Secondary flight controls improve aircraft performance characteristics and consist of high lift devices such as flaps, slats, spoilers, and trim systems designed to relieve excessive control forces. See the diagram on the next page.

LEARNING TO FLY - ESSENTIAL ELEMENTS

Primary Flight Controls

- Elevator: produces and controls pitch—the nose moves toward or away from you.
- Aileron: produces and controls roll—the wing moves toward or away from the landing gear.
- Rudder: controls and prevents adverse yaw—yaw is movement of the nose toward the wingtip.

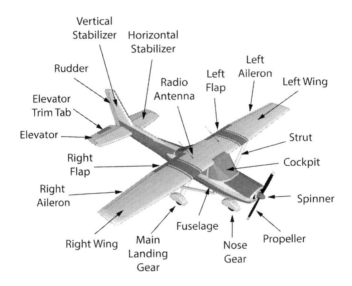

Secondary Flight Controls

- Trim: holds control surfaces (rudder, elevator, and ailerons) in a specific position.
- Flaps: (Krueger, Fowler, Slotted, Slats)—high lift devices used to reduce the stalling speed of an aircraft wing at given weight.
- Spoilers: devices on the wing that "spoil," or **reduce**, the lift being made, adding drag to help slow down the aircraft during flight. Ground spoilers are used during landing to help stop the aircraft. Be advised that very few light aircraft have spoilers.

Flight Controls

Flight Controls Brief

An understanding of Aircraft Flight Controls is necessary to master the **Four Fundamentals of Flight: Straight and Level, Turns, Climbs, and Descents** (ch. 5). On Day-One, the student should be able to master the turn (sec. 5.2). It is imperative to know that none of the controls directly turn an aircraft. The coordinated application of ailerons and rudder will set an attitude—specifically, a bank—which allows the aircraft to begin its turn. Once the bank is established, the lift generated by the wing turns the aircraft.

We control the amount of lift generated by the wing, whether climbing, level, or descending, by varying the Angle of Attack (AOA), the angle at which relative wind meets an airfoil (wing), with the elevator or horizontal stabilizer. Keep in mind, the turn is made in conjunction with any of the other three fundamentals of flight: level, climbing, or descending. Once a roll is begun with the ailerons, the nose will yaw in the opposite direction **(Adverse Yaw)** unless an appropriate amount of rudder is applied in the direction of the roll.

Why does this happen? Rolling to the right, the right aileron goes up, and your left aileron goes down. Lowering the left aileron changes the **Chord Line**, an imaginary straight line joining the leading edge and the trailing edge of an airfoil (wing), creating a higher AOA.

Chord Line

As AOA increases, Lift also increases. When Lift increases, Induced Drag also increases. Remember, Induced Drag always happens when you are creating Lift. The drag will pull the wing to the left. **Proverse Yaw** (with rudder) is needed for correction. After all, you want the nose to be moving in the same direction as your turn. Once the bank is established and the ailerons are neutralized, Adverse Yaw is no longer being produced, thus rudder is not necessary.

When it's time to roll out of the turn, banking the aircraft (ailerons) will again create **Adverse Yaw** unless an appropriate amount of rudder is applied in the direction of the rollout. In other words, in a coordinated turn, adverse yaw is countered by using the rudder. Adding rudder input creates a side force on the vertical tail that opposes adverse yaw.

Moreover, while in a bank, if you stop the turn with the rudder only (poor technique), the aircraft will roll out of the bank because of the Dihedral (below image) of the wing.

Dihedral

In a bank, the bottom (lower) wing has a higher AOA than the top (higher) wing, thus the low wing will rise.

To begin a turn, one should never try to roll an aircraft with only the rudder; it begins the roll indirectly and very inefficiently through the wings. If your nose is pointed straight up with little or no aileron-effectiveness, then the rudder is the only thing you've got. Now you're in an **Unusual Attitude** (ch. 11). Full rudder, with help from mother nature (gravity), should easily get your nose down for a quick recovery.

Dihedral Angle is a design feature that helps improve stability, especially when rolling left or right. It's the upward angle of the wings (or tail surface) from a horizontal axis, and it increases lateral stability in a

Flight Controls

bank by causing the lower wing to fly at a higher AOA than the higher wing. This design varies depending on the aircraft, but not all aircraft have this built-in advantage. Some have Anhedral wings which are tilted downward at the outer tips, but most high-wing aircraft have Dihedral wings.

Use of the horizon as a Focal Reference Point is crucial in the beginning stages of learning the Four Fundamentals of Flight.

Ninety percent of what a pilot does is setting an attitude with the Flight Controls. The key is knowing which controls to use and where to look. Becoming familiar with the flight controls during flight, while may be challenging on the student's first flight, will be quickly mastered.

Referencing the horizon with each application of the controls, while performing Straight and Level Flight, Turns, Climbs, or Descents, **(The Four Fundamentals)**, is the key habit-pattern to learn from Day-One. These precise procedures should never change throughout a pilot's career, regardless of the aircraft type.

Trim should never be applied too quickly when transitioning to a different attitude.

Aircraft Trim is an adjustable section that applies a force on a control surface (like the elevator) to keep it in position. It works by redirecting airflow just like the control surface itself. This means that the pilot does not have to constantly apply a force on the yoke to keep the control surface in position.

Set the attitude with the Flight Controls and allow the aircraft to stabilize at the next attitude before attempting to Trim Out the control pressures. Some instructors recommend counting five seconds after the new attitude is set before trimming out the control pressures.

> The important take-away here is to never fly the aircraft with the Trim Wheel or Trim Switch. This is the job of the Primary Flight Controls.

Chapter 5
Four Fundamentals of Flight

> The Four Fundamentals: Straight and Level Flight, Turns, Climbs, and Descents are the basic flight maneuvers that enable pilots to navigate and control the aircraft.

Every maneuver executed from an aircraft includes at least one or more of the Four Fundamentals of Flight. For instance, Straight and Level is accomplished by visually checking the lateral-level relationship between the natural horizon and the wingtips, then performing adjustments (roll) as needed to maintain a straight heading. This lateral-level relationship is one of two interpretations of the term "Level." (More on this later.)

Many times, introductory flight lessons do not stress the importance of looking primarily outside the aircraft, referencing the glareshield, when changing between each of the four fundamentals of flight. Over the years, I have witnessed pilots having their eyes predominantly inside the aircraft as the primary response to begin an attitude change, when in fact, their first response should be to maneuver the aircraft while looking outside the aircraft.

Being adequately trained in attitude flying from the beginning would have produced a thoroughly ingrained habit to set the attitude first, referencing the glareshield against the horizon. Once the attitude is set, there is plenty of time to fine-tune the number you are trying to achieve with a quick glance at the appropriate instrument.

The concept of learning to fly and recognizing the attitudes of the aircraft (looking outside) may seem like an insignificant perception for some people; however, the majority of feedback, which has become common knowledge in the aviation community, is that pilots keep their heads in the cockpit too much. This observation, coupled with an unacceptable aircraft accident rate, is a strong reason to rethink the importance of this basic concept.

When queried about the four fundamentals of flight, many of the responses I have received over the years from all types of pilot backgrounds have been **"Lift, Drag, Thrust, and Gravity."** Of course, this answer is incorrect, and is, in fact, the response to the question: What are the **Four Forces** acting on an aircraft?

5.1 Straight and Level

Now is a good time to clearly define Straight vs Level for the student pilot. Straight means the heading (compass) and the Directional Gyro (DG) are not moving. If they are moving, you are not straight. Level means the altimeter is not moving. If it is moving, you are not Level.

The word "Level" has two connotations. Flying is in three dimensions. Rolling the aircraft around the longitudinal axis allows the aircraft to fly straight by keeping the wings level, as well as placing the aircraft in a bank. Since the majority of flying is in Straight and Level Flight, it's important to understand the word "Level," in this context, means maintaining an attitude around the lateral (pitch) axis that prevents the altimeter from moving, the altimeter being the primary instrument for Level Flight. When the altimeter is not moving, you are Level.

Four Fundamentals of Flight

The images below provide a "bird's-eye" view of the four attitudes associated with the Four Fundamentals of Flight. The Student Pilot needs to thoroughly know and understand the procedures needed to confidently manipulate the aircraft and engine controls through each fundamental of flight.

The goal should be an **"Automatic Response"** utilizing the pilot's senses of sight, sound, and touch. The following pages specifically detail how to perform each maneuver, emphasizing when, how, where, and why with each scenario.

Top Image: left to right
Climb Attitude (top of glareshield on the horizon)
Straight and Level (top of glareshield inches below the horizon)
Descent Attitude (top of glareshield well below the horizon)

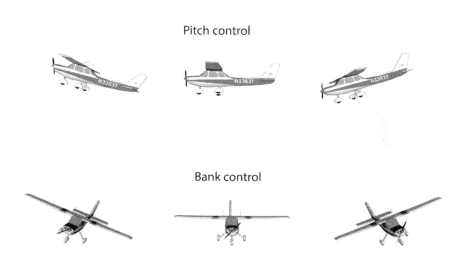

Bottom Image: left to right
Left Turn and Level
Straight and Level
Right Turn and Level

LEARNING TO FLY - ESSENTIAL ELEMENTS

Learning to fly Straight and Level requires knowing when and where to look while moving the controls.

Referencing the glareshield with the horizon to find the "sweet spot" that keeps the altimeter from moving is the ultimate goal. Occasionally glancing, but never staring, at the altimeter immediately provides the information you need to make the necessary pitch change.

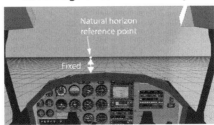

Level Flight Attitude-No Flaps

Because experienced pilots have trained themselves to look outside the aircraft the majority of the time, small changes in attitude are immediately noticed. Cross-checking the altimeter to stay level should be a constant but relaxed procedure.

5.2 Day-One Turn

- **Left Turn.** Look right, through center, then left.

- **Right Turn.** Look left, through center, then right.

    These looks should be deliberate, encompassing both:
    (1) traffic clearing
    (2) ensuring the desired aircraft attitude: climb, level or descent.

- **Pick a Ground Reference Point in Front of the Wing (90 degrees).** Make a conscious effort to remember your ground reference point here.

Four Fundamentals of Flight

- **Head and Eyes Forward.** This is a critical point. Drivers do not stare out of the right or left side of cars while turning. So why do I see pilots fixate away from what they should be doing, which is flying the aircraft. This is especially prevalent on downwind just prior to turning to base when I observe pilots staring back at the runway. In the meantime, the nose is all over the place. Your head should be on a swivel, and it's okay to look quickly, but flying the aircraft (aircraft attitude in pitch and roll) is paramount.

- **Roll Smoothly into 30 Degrees of Bank with Coordinated Aileron and Rudder.** Once established in the bank, neutralize the aileron roll control. Use slight back elevator pressure to maintain the desired attitude (climb, level, or descent).

- **Maintain the Desired Pitch Attitude and Bank** while scanning for traffic (head on a swivel).

- **When the Ground Reference Point is in Sight,** roll out slightly beyond the point.

At no time does this procedure negate the fact that your head should always be on a swivel for ***"See and Avoid."**

The idiom "Head on a Swivel" originates from the military. Imagine a radar system continuously scanning its surroundings for potential threats. Pilots must do the same.

Day-One Turn Brief

When thinking about the horizon, most people visualize a half circle with the horizon on the bottom and the sky above. Pilots, however, think about the horizon on the top with the earth below. The horizon is always level with the pilot's eye from the surface to 50,000 feet. All

---

* **"See and Avoid"** is a method for avoiding collision requiring that pilots should actively search for potentially conflicting traffic, especially when operating in airspace where all traffic is not operating under ATC instructions.

LEARNING TO FLY - ESSENTIAL ELEMENTS

Straight and Level Flight, Turns, Climbs, and Descents are referenced from this vantage point.

It's important that pilots know how to recognize the Pitch Attitude for each fundamental of flight.

When looking outside, we are trained to reference the top of the glareshield above the aircraft instrument panel in relation to the horizon.

- Straight and Level is represented with the glareshield being placed a certain distance below the horizon. That distance is about the same for every aircraft, including jets. We should master the straight and level attitude first during normal cruise maneuvering.

- The Climb Attitude is represented with the aircraft pitched up with the top of the glareshield on the horizon.

- The Descent Attitude is represented with the glareshield being placed farther below the level attitude in reference to the horizon. This descent position will vary depending upon the amount of flaps being extended.

- The Turn Attitude (bank) incorporates any of the other three fundamentals: Straight and Level, Climbs, or Descents.

So, how does one determine the precise Straight and Level Pitch Attitude? Three steps:

1. Glance at the primary instrument for Level Flight, the Altimeter.
2. Find the attitude that stops the Altimeter from moving.
3. Then, carefully gauge the distance outside the aircraft from the horizon to the glareshield.

Memorize that distance in your mind's eye. Descent attitudes are determined similarly with enroute descents clean, meaning no flaps, and

Four Fundamentals of Flight

landing approaches, meaning one-half and full flaps. Being able to place the aircraft quickly and smoothly at the appropriately desired attitude is a great first start.

After stabilized in the proper attitude, with all the procedures completed for each maneuver, you will then have time to fine-tune the attitude, referencing the primary instruments: **Altimeter** for Level Flight, **Airspeed** for Pitch, and **Directional Gyro** for Bank.

Again, the "Day-One Turn" can include a Climb, Level (altitude), or Descent (attitude), regardless of flap position.

I must mention one point that I believe is most important for a beginning student: a normal turn incorporates 30 degrees of bank. Defined as a medium bank by the FAA, anything less is inappropriate.

If you are a student reading this brief and your instructor trains you to use 15 or 20 degrees of bank during your maneuvers or while in the traffic pattern, your instructor is doing you a disservice. It is important for the student to learn and master the feel and attitude sight picture of a normal 30 degree-bank turn during climb, level, or descent attitudes from the very beginning.

An argument has been made to limit inexperienced pilots to 20 degrees of bank until they gain more experience. Some examiners are uncomfortable with inexperienced pilots using more than 20 degrees of bank for a normal turn during a checkride, but students who have been taught to use only 15 to 20 degrees of bank find themselves having the plane fly them instead of them flying the plane. Recognize that you control the plane; the plane does not control you.

I believe the issue is Pitch Attitude and not Bank.

If the student is adequately taught **Attitude Flying**, 30 degrees of bank should be no issue. Of course, smaller bank angles and lower pitch attitudes will be necessary to compensate for departing high-elevation airports or any high-density altitude scenario where aircraft and engine performance may be degraded or marginal.

LEARNING TO FLY - ESSENTIAL ELEMENTS

Why 30 degrees of bank? Two Reasons:

1. Thirty degrees is a Normal, Medium-Bank Turn. This is the one you will be using for the rest of your flying career. Every pilot in the world uses it in the traffic pattern, with jets or GA aircraft. We do this to ensure our turn radius is acceptable for the traffic pattern. Your lateral separation (turning room) should be about the same distance on downwind at every airport, but always consider the wind because the lateral distance may change. I usually place a piece of tape on the strut or wing for the student to use as a reference from the runway for the correct distance.

2. Thirty degrees of bank allows the pilot to make the turn in a timely fashion for "See and Avoid" considerations. Always consider the amount of heading-change needed before you make the turn. Do not use more than 30 degrees of bank for any turn that exceeds 30 degrees of heading-change. If turning 40 degrees, you should still use only a max of 30 degrees of bank. Otherwise, if less than 30 degrees of heading-change, you should match the number of degrees of desired turn with the number of degrees of bank.

Example: If you want to turn 15 degrees, you use 15 degrees of bank, five would be five, two would be two, 10 would be 10, etc.

Something to consider while in a left turn as opposed to a right turn is a slight change in the position of the horizon in relation to the glareshield. A left turn will place the student pilot, assuming he/she is in the left seat, in a slightly lower position than the pilot in the right seat because of the rotation around the longitudinal axis of the aircraft.

Conversely, a right turn will place the student slightly higher than the other pilot. Informed of and trained in this information, the pilot will naturally recalibrate his/her horizon-reference point while in the turn whether climbing, level, or descending.

Four Fundamentals of Flight

It's easier in a level turn to gauge the horizon position, so start there before mastering the climb and descent attitudes. Simply maintain the pitch attitude that allows the altimeter to not move and note the horizon position in relation to the glareshield (sight picture).

Speaking of Sight Picture, from Day-One, the idea of memorizing the turn-bank attitude of 30 degrees without staring at the attitude gyro, referencing the horizon in relation to the glareshield, will also bear good fruit. Additionally, it is crucial to brief the student on how to maintain level flight by glancing, but not staring, at the altimeter and the horizon when making small pitch adjustments to keep the altimeter from moving.

From the outset, a good pilot is keen on noticing every little pitch and bank movement, noting but not staring at the flight instruments. The pilot's attention should be primarily focused **outside the aircraft**. This is critical in all phases of flight, especially in the landing phase. These concepts *must* be briefed and taught.

The Day-One Turn, also known as a Normal VFR Turn, or Clearing Turn, is a necessary tool for the student/pilot.

I use the term "Day-One" because a student should have learned this on the first day. Learning/performing this procedure the same way every time is a positive and confidence-building habit. I emphasize that in no way does this procedure abrogate the student's responsibility to **"See and Avoid."** Again, your head should always be on a swivel.

How Airplanes Turn

During Straight and Level Flight, the downwash created by the shape of the wing causes the lift force to act vertically to push the aircraft upward. Banking the aircraft tilts this lifting force, pulling the aircraft in the direction of the banked turn.

Technically, it's this horizontal component of lift that turns an aircraft. Setting a banked attitude will allow lift to turn an aircraft.

Less lift is available in the banked attitude against the aircraft weight due to forces caused by acceleration. Acceleration is defined as a change in speed or direction.

Without applying back pressure and increasing the AOA to create lift, the aircraft will descend.

Increasing the AOA with back pressure on the yoke/stick also increases total drag, which slows down the aircraft.

The Effects of Total Lift

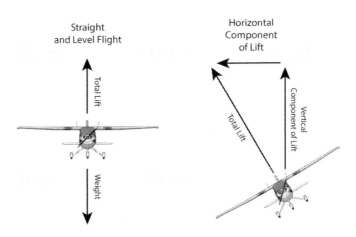

A normal, medium-banked turn of 30 degrees isn't a speed concern for the pilot; however, steep turns in excess of 45 degrees will require more power to maintain airspeed.

Remember, never commence a turn without conscientiously selecting and remembering a reference point on your wing before the turn. All the steps for the "Day-One Turn" are there for a reason and will provide you confidence and promote safety in your flying days ahead.

Four Fundamentals of Flight

5.3 Climb and Level Off + High Performance (HP)

Climb

- Nose to the Climb Attitude
- Full Power
- Check Speed ____ Knots
- Trim for the Climb Attitude

Level Off

- Nose to the Level Attitude
- Airspeed to Cruise ____ Knots
- Power to Cruise Revolutions per Minute (RPM)
- Trim
- Lean the Mixture

Climb HP

- Nose to the Climb Attitude
- Full Power: Mixture Enrich as desired, Prop 2500 to 2600 RPM, Throttle Push to Top of Green Arc, Cowl Flaps Open as Desired
- Check Speed ___ Knots
- Trim for the Climb Attitude

Level Off HP

- Nose to the Level Attitude
- Airspeed to Cruise ___ Knots
- Power: Throttle within the Green Arc, Prop 2300 to 2500 RPM, Cowl Flaps Closed
- Trim
- Lean the Mixture

LEARNING TO FLY - ESSENTIAL ELEMENTS

High Performance (HP): Aircraft with engines capable of developing more than 200 horsepower. These procedures also cover the features of Complex Aircraft, meaning aircraft with retractable landing gear, flaps, and controllable pitch propeller.

Climb and Level Off Brief

From Day-One, it is essential that pilots learn Attitude Flying, keeping one important thing in mind: you do not fly with the Trim Wheel; you fly with the yoke, stick, whichever you have.

You do this by first setting an attitude with the yoke. Once the attitude is set and the aircraft is stabilized with the Airspeed Indicator (the primary instrument for pitch), you then begin trimming the control pressures out until the aircraft can fly hands off. Trimming is analogous to the steering wheel in a car: while driving, the steering wheel acts as a Trim Wheel, providing small corrections to stay on the road.

Trimming an Aircraft acts in the same way to maintain the desired attitude you are attempting to set. Above 10,000-feet altitude, where performance is degraded, it is better to add the power first, then slowly rotate the pitch to the climb attitude. The same thing applies to jets above 10,000 feet: add power first to maintain your speed, then transition to the climb. But below 10,000-feet altitude, climb attitude comes first, and then add power.

Let's Review:

The Climb Attitude results by placing the top of the glareshield on or slightly above the horizon, utilizing smooth elevator-control input, then adding power.

Once the aircraft has stabilized in pitch and power (it takes time for the aircraft to slow to climb speed), small adjustments can be made in pitch to provide you with the desired climb airspeed.

Four Fundamentals of Flight

Now is the time to note how much elevator trim is required to maintain the climb attitude. At the stabilized climb airspeed, count the number of turns it requires on the trim wheel to maintain this pitch attitude while looking outside.

Remember, airspeed is the primary instrument for pitch; however, do not stare at the gauge—a quick glance is all that is necessary. Your primary focus should be looking outside, referencing the horizon and the glareshield.

I maintain the order in which you perform the climb transition while below 10,000 feet is necessary to understand what the aircraft is about to do. Placing the aircraft in the Climb Attitude first is essential before beginning anything else. Professional pilots know how much trim it takes for a climb, a level off, and a descent.

Climb Attitude

The Level Off from a Climb or Descent is basically the same procedure. Learn immediately how much trim you need for the three attitudes—Climb, Level, and Descent—and you are on the road to flying with confidence and proficiency.

Leveling off from a Normal Climb following the procedures in section 5.3 may require some explanation:

When leveling off in a HP aircraft, do not reduce the power until within 1000 to 500 feet of your desired altitude, depending on your rate of climb. Establish a reduced climb attitude while trimming, resulting in a 500-feet (or less) rate of climb.

LEARNING TO FLY - ESSENTIAL ELEMENTS

This applies to jets and HP aircraft. Of course, if you are climbing at 5000 feet-per-minute in a lightly-loaded HP jet, you will need to reduce the power much earlier to achieve that 500-feet rate of climb.

Reducing the power allows a HP aircraft to imitate what a light-aircraft trainer should be doing within 1000 feet of level off. That is, 500 feet-per-minute or less.

* * *

The rest of the procedure is the same for all aircraft.

At Level Off, now the pitch change requires only about two or three degrees, which is hardly noticeable in any aircraft, including jets.

Do not begin the Level Off by pushing the nose over to the level attitude until you get to the desired altitude, referencing the altimeter (the primary instrument for level flight), or you'll never get there! This is assuming you have the rate of climb below 500 feet-per-minute by appropriately managing the power.

The aircraft will immediately stop climbing once the two-degree pitch change is made. It will now take a few seconds to accelerate to cruise airspeed. Continue the level-off procedure, not reducing the power until you reach cruise airspeed, then power, trim, and lean the mixture. At this time, you can count the number of times it takes rotating the Trim Wheel. This gives you an idea of how many revolutions it takes.

Maintain altitude (altimeter) with the flight control yoke, glancing inside at the altimeter while referencing the horizon by looking outside the aircraft. Scan back and forth. If the altimeter moves, stop it from moving by making the appropriate pitch change with the yoke, being careful not to fly with the Trim Wheel.

It's important to never stare at a moving altimeter; it tells you nothing while it is moving.

Four Fundamentals of Flight

Remember, Do Not Fly with the Trim Wheel. You are always setting and adjusting the yoke to maintain the attitude and the altitude. The Trim Wheel is to be used only to neutralize the control pressures to set the attitude.

If you are taking more than a few seconds to level off, you are doing something wrong.

I've witnessed pilots taking five minutes or more to level off because they began the procedure many feet below the desired altitude and reduced the power too soon, never really getting to the altitude and airspeed they desired. This is simply because they did not understand attitude flying and what was happening in a level off. This procedure needs to be trained and understood.

* * *

The 10 Percent Rule is an alternative method of leveling off from a climb used by many instructors.

For example, a 500-foot rate of climb would mean beginning the level off at 50 feet. I find this procedure unnecessary because the two-degree pitch change at the final level-off altitude, necessary for the level off, immediately stops the climb. Overcorrecting the pitch change by even a degree or two, 50 feet below the level-off altitude, only lengthens the time to level off and increases the workload.

Waiting until the aircraft arrives at the desired altitude, performing the appropriate pitch change, and monitoring the attitude and altimeter, simplifies the entire procedure. The minute pitch change is hardly noticeable and immediately stops the climb. All that is left to do is maintain altitude as the aircraft accelerates, then reduce the power at the desired cruise speed.

5.4 Descents and Level Off: Enroute, Terminal, Final Approach + HP Procedures

Enroute Descents (constant speed)

- Reduce Power to 2000 RPM
- Lower Nose to the Descent Attitude
- Check Speed ____ Descent Cruise Speed
- Trim for the Descent Attitude

Level Off

- Raise Nose to the Level Attitude
- Airspeed to Cruise
- Power
- Trim
- Lean the Mixture

Enroute Descents HP (Constant Speed)

- Reduce Power: Mixture Enrich as desired, Throttle Reduce
- Lower Nose to the Descent Attitude
- Check Speed ___ Descent Cruise Speed
- Trim

Level Off HP

- Raise Nose to the Level Attitude
- Airspeed to Cruise
- Power: 22 to 24 Inches as Desired
- Trim
- Lean the Mixture

Four Fundamentals of Flight

Final Approach Descent from the *Abeam Position or Straight In: regardless of flap position, this procedure will be used for both the stall series and the slip profiles

- Mixture Rich, Fuel Pump On
- Carb Heat On, Power 1500 RPM
- Maintain Level Altitude (altimeter does not move)
- TRIM
- Flaps: First Notch, Landing Gear Down
- At 80 knots, Nose to the Descent Attitude
- **GUMPS**, Landing Checklist Complete (see checklist below)
- Day-One Turn, Second Notch of Flaps while in the Turn (75 kts)
- On Base After Rollout, Ask Yourself: High or Low? (aiming point) Make Corrections Early (power/flaps)
- Day-One Turn onto Final
- When Aiming Point and Runway (glideslope) Ensured, Full Flaps
- Target Airspeed, (70 knots) Descent Attitude / TA = Vso x 1.3 + Wind Additive
- Maintain Aiming Point, Line Up, Airspeed Vref (65 kts) Over the Threshold
- Do Not Raise the Nose (descent attitude) Until You Are Ready to Land
- **The Go-Around Procedure** must be used out of this configuration

GUMPS CHECKLIST

Gas: fuel on the proper tank, pump on/off as required
Undercarriage: landing gear up/down as required
Mixture: set
Prop (s): set
Safety items

---

* **Abeam:** touchdown point is 90 degrees to the left/right of the track of your aircraft.

LEARNING TO FLY - ESSENTIAL ELEMENTS

The **"GUMPS"** mental checklist plays a pivotal roll in the pre-landing routine. It is a quick and effective way to double-check critical pieces of the landing checklist.

Final Approach HP Descent from the *Abeam Position or Straight In: regardless of flap position, this procedure will be used for both the stall series and the slip profiles

- Mixture Rich, Carb Heat On, Power 16 inches Manifold Pressure (MP), Prop Full Forward
- Maintain Level Flight (altimeter does not move)
- TRIM
- Flaps: First Notch, Landing Gear Down, Power 1600 RPM
- At 80 kts, Nose to the Descent Attitude
- **GUMPS**, Landing Checklist Complete
- Day-One Turn
- Second Notch of Flaps
- On Base after Rollout, Ask Yourself High or Low? (aiming point). Make Corrections Early (power/flaps)
- Day-One Turn onto Final
- When Aiming Point/Runway (glideslope) Ensured, Full Flaps
- At 70 Kts, Maintain Aiming Point, Line up, Airspeed. Power Idle in the Flare
- **Perform the Go-Around Procedure**, if necessary

Descents Brief

There are actually four types of Descents: Enroute, Terminal Approach, Final Approach, and Emergency (sec. 17.2). Descents are executed because of several reasons. Air Traffic Control (ATC) requests for descent are mandatory and must be complied with regardless of whether you're flying by Visual Flight Rules (VFR) or on an Instrument Flight Rules (IFR) clearance. Rough air turbulence is used frequently by the pilot for shorter or longer descents. Of course, transi-

---

* **Abeam:** touchdown point is 90 degrees to the left/right of the track of your aircraft.

Four Fundamentals of Flight

tioning from a cruise altitude in order to enter the Terminal and Final Approach Phases is the most obvious reason to commence a descent.

Enroute Descents

Planning a descent encompassing an enroute portion, followed by a terminal and final approach descent, requires knowing how and when to create a flight path.

I'll first discuss jets for those students heading for the airlines or military.

Referencing the Instantaneous Vertical Speed Indicator (IVSI), slowly engage the autopilot using the Vertical Speed, Vertical Navigation (VNAV), or Flight Level Change to begin a 500 to 1000 feet-per-minute rate of descent.

Slightly reduce power to maintain your Cruise Mach Number (usually between .7 to .88 for most jets).

Establish a rate of descent between 1000 to 1500 feet-per-minute until arriving at your indicated descent speed (usually between 280 knots to 330 knots) depending on your aircraft.

Maintain your speed, **throttle at idle**, around 1500 to 2000 feet-per-minute IVSI until reaching 10,000 feet, at which time level off with power to idle and slow to 250 knots. After that, it's generally an **idle descent** until you enter the terminal phase of the descent.

The **"How"** part is simple. Vertical Speed and throttle are primary to maintain your airspeed. Always take note of the attitude of the aircraft in relation to the horizon as you are descending.

If Instrument Meteorological Conditions (IMC) exist, note the attitude on the Attitude Directional Indicator (ADI). It's the **"When"** part that is the challenge.

The **"When"** part consists of creating a flight path in your head so you can commence the descent to arrive at your final destination at the appropriate time. Calculate a path that places the aircraft through a

LEARNING TO FLY - ESSENTIAL ELEMENTS

window 30 miles from the airport at 10,000 feet. Use a three-to-one or two-to-one ratio to calculate this path.

While at Cruise Altitude, determine how many thousands of feet you need to lose to arrive at the window: 10,000 feet at 30 miles from the airport.

Example: Cruising at 37,000 feet, subtract 10,000 from 37,000; this gives you 27,000 feet to lose. Multiply that by three; this gives you a three-to-one ratio: 3 x 27 = 81. So, 81 miles to the first window plus 30 miles to the airport equals 111 miles. This is when to begin your descent.

Your **Descent Rate** should be around 1500 feet-per-minute. As you descend, you can continue to update your three-to-one calculation and adjust your descent rate to maintain the path.

A two-to-one is much steeper and requires a 3000 feet per minute or more descent rate. It's also a much faster airspeed. Some pilots like to fly fast, although, it's not very fuel efficient. You derive a two-to-one in the same manner.

Planning a descent for GA light aircraft is very similar.

Because light aircraft may be unpressurized, avoid high descent rates to ensure passenger comfort. A 500 feet-per-minute descent rate can be mathematically calculated based on how many thousands of feet you need to lose. Two minutes per 1000 feet is an easy method once you determine how much altitude to lose.

Knowing your groundspeed in miles-per-minute, you can determine the time/distance from which to descend. I reference the end point of the descent at five miles from the airport at airport pattern altitude unless there are obstacle-clearance considerations.

Four Fundamentals of Flight

Phoenix Skyharbor Airport VFR approach from the east is a good example. There are many mountains not visible at night between you and the airport. Descent to pattern altitude would not be appropriate in this scenario.

A three-to-one ratio can also be used, just like jets. Determine the altitude to lose in thousands of feet to pattern altitude, multiply by three and begin your descent at that distance.

Example: With Cruise Alt at 7500 feet and Pattern Alt at 1500 feet, subtract 1500 from 7500; this gives you 6000 feet to lose: 3 x 6 = 18 miles. Add five miles for the distance end point of the descent from the airport. Consider the winds with a starting point of 23 miles from the airport. Descent at 500 to 1000 feet-per-minute.

Winds *do* affect a descent, so it's necessary to recalculate the numbers as you descend. With today's advent of VNAV on the Flight Management Computers, all the calculations are done for the pilot.

I would strongly recommend you utilize the mental calculation above every time you descend to back up any VNAV calculations. It's a good Situational-Awareness (SA) exercise to keep you fresh and in the game.

Terminal Approach Descents

Once you have arrived at the first window (30 nm, 250 kts, 10,000 feet), descent now encompasses the Terminal Phase of the flight. Your next goal should be to arrive at the next window **(second window approach phase)** on speed and at an appropriate altitude to be able to commence a normal descent to landing.

From 30 miles, all aircraft—jets or piston—continue at the appropriate speed for their type aircraft to comply with Class B (250-kts max),

LEARNING TO FLY - ESSENTIAL ELEMENTS

Class D (200-kts max) to arrive at the second approach window, which is defined as either a Straight-In Final Approach Fix (FAF) or modified base, or abeam the touchdown point, at pattern altitude or FAF altitude, whichever is applicable. The second window defines the position where the aircraft must be fully configured for landing, full flaps and gear, landing checks complete.

Arriving at the FAF, or the traffic pattern, requires a speed reduction. For jets, minimum maneuvering speeds are already calculated and provided for each flap setting and are bugged on the airspeed indicator. This calculation is termed the Defined Minimum Maneuver Speed (DMMS).

For GA aircraft, take your stall speed <u>clean</u> (Vs1), multiply it by 1.404, which will give you your clean DMMS speed for maneuvering in the traffic pattern. I strongly recommend you bug your clean DMMS speed. This provides a safe speed around the pattern for most of your maneuvering. It is not necessary to bug all flap-setting DMMS speeds in GA aircraft as opposed to airline operations.

GA defines maneuver speed (Va) as the maximum speed selected by the aircraft designer. At speeds close to or faster than maneuver speed (Va), full deflection of the flight-control surfaces should not be attempted because of the risk of aircraft structural damage. Notice that **Va** is a <u>maximum</u> speed. **DMMS** is a <u>minimum</u> speed.

Va and DMMS are two different concepts. Va comes from the GA Community; DMMS comes from the Airline Community and is used to mitigate reduced airspeed issues associated with maneuvering during the departure and approach phases of the flight.

By calculating DMMS for GA aircraft, pilots can enjoy a much better level of safety. I would encourage pilots to bug their airspeed indicator with their Vref speed (Vso x 1.3) and their DMMS speed (Vs1 x 1.404). Once you are fully configured and on Final to land, you would transition from the DMMS speed to the Vref speed calculation.

Four Fundamentals of Flight

To recap, we calculate this by multiplying the Landing-Flap-Stall-Speed (Vso) by 1.3. This calculation is your Vref speed. This is *not* the speed you fly on final approach. Why? Because it is not permitted to fly even one knot below Vref until you are in the flare, ready to land.

Allow yourself a little breathing room by calculating a **Target Speed**. Add five knots to Vref for any approach with less than 10 knots of reported wind. This is your **Target Speed** and the speed you would fly. Any wind more than 10 knots would require recalculating a new target speed accounting for the increased winds. This applies to all aircraft.

There are several ways to consider a wind additive, but whatever you decide to use, the calculation should never be more than 20 knots above Vref for any aircraft. At our major airline, we calculated one-half the wind plus the gust added to Vref speed, not to exceed 20 knots.

Caution: Never add a wind additive to your target speed, only to the Vref speed. There are other ways to calculate a wind additive provided by aviation authors, but this is the one we used.

Knowing your clean **DMMS**, **Vref**, and **Target** speeds, and especially your attitude awareness of the aircraft, will protect you in the traffic pattern. Pilots who are oblivious to these protections are "accidents waiting to happen."

Since Descents always encompass one of the Four Fundaments of Flight, it's important to know and understand the "Descent Attitude-Sight Picture."

As a professional pilot, you should be keenly aware of the Descent Attitude-Sight Picture both inside (ADI) and outside (Horizon). Always focus on that Sight Picture during your descent, regardless of the configuration. Just like climbing or straight and level or turning, learn what to expect regardless of the aircraft configuration.

LEARNING TO FLY - ESSENTIAL ELEMENTS

As the pilot is seated, all attitude changes are accomplished by referencing the top of the glareshield. Utilizing the flight controls, the pilot must develop a keen awareness as to the appropriate placement of the glareshield in relation to the horizon. The images below show the aircraft Descent Attitudes as you would expect to see them in the half flaps and full flaps descent attitude configurations.

Descent Attitude-Half Flaps

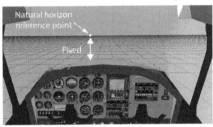

Descent Attitude-Full Flaps

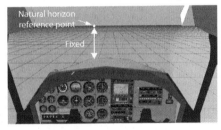

* * *

A thorough knowledge and understanding of the Four Fundamentals of Flight, and the accompanying procedures, as discussed in this chapter should provide pilots a strong foundation as they navigate through their aviation journey. Couple this important knowledge with disciplined practice, always completing the procedures the same way every time and building solid habit-patterns, will bear good fruit

Chapter 6
The Go-Around Procedure

> The high number of "messed-up" Go-Arounds with unfortunate consequences substantiates the need to place this procedure at the top of a pilot's priority in training and proficiency.

Many pilots feel that the need to perform a Go-Around during the landing phase indicates a lack of skill, or it is evidence that they somehow "messed up." This idea, of course, is purely psychological and needs a paradigm shift. A Go-Around should be viewed as a corrective measure and a potentially life-saving maneuver, not as a critique on your piloting skills.

In my experience, GA treats the Go-Around Procedure as an afterthought; however, it should be treated as the most important resource in a pilot's toolkit. It is among the riskiest maneuvers in aviation because there is little margin for error—it needs to be practiced to proficiency.

Go-Arounds are taught in relation to the runway and landing phase of flight; but in reality, the Go-Around Procedure has nothing to do with the runway or approach and everything to do with placing the aircraft in a known, safe, flying state. During the initial flight-training stage, I can think of five times a Go-Around Procedure should be demonstrated and performed, and this occurs nowhere near the ground, much less a runway. Anytime the aircraft is placed in the landing configuration, a Go-Around Procedure would be the recovery maneuver. I offer examples of this in the Go-Around Procedure brief at the end of this chapter.

On approach to land, one needs to think about and guard against "Planned Continuation Bias," the unconscious cognitive bias to continue with the original plan in spite of changing conditions. It is a serious threat when you disregard unsafe conditions and proceed to approach and land anyway; when in reality, the safer choice would be to perform the Go-Around Procedure.

Go-Around Procedure

- Full Power, *Carb Heat Off
- Airspeed in the Green
- Nose to the Climb Attitude
- Flaps Up in Increments (flap handle to takeoff-flap setting)
- †Positive Rate, Gear Up, Cowl Flaps Open
- Remaining Flaps Up, After Takeoff Checklist

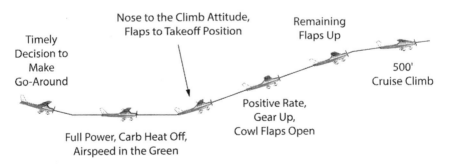

---

* **Carb Heat** is aligned with step one because it is a function of power. Never think about power without thinking about carb heat.
† **Positive Rate** implies two positive climb indications: (1) Altimeter, (2) Vertical Speed.

The Go-Around Procedure

The Go-Around Procedure Brief

So, what are the scenarios when a Go-Around Procedure would be considered? The obvious scenario is a situation on final approach where a landing is not feasible for a variety of reasons. What needs to be addressed are other situations not so obvious to many pilots.

For one example, the Go-Around Procedure should be utilized **after recovery** (stick forward) from any stall. Once the AOA is reduced below the Critical Angle of Attack (C-AOA) and the wings are flying again, the Go-Around Procedure, executed properly, will place the aircraft in a known, safe, flying state. The airlines, Flight Safety and CAE routinely train this procedure.

ATC can request that an aircraft go around, perhaps when there isn't enough spacing or when a collision might be possible.

Additionally, Slow Flight, regardless of the configuration and speed, requires the use of the Go-Around Procedure to return the aircraft to a known, safe, flying state. The only exception here, of course, is to maintain altitude (nose to the **level** attitude instead of the **climb** attitude) during recovery to normal flying speed.

Anytime the aircraft is somehow placed in an unknown flying state, such as a startled effect from an **Unusual Attitude Event**, the Go-Around Procedure is your go-to tool once you have stabilized the aircraft. Also, recovery from Sideslip or Forward Slip demonstrations require a Go-Around Procedure. Again, anytime the aircraft needs to be placed in a known, safe, flying state, your go-to recovery is the Go-Around Procedure.

A student pilot should never be permitted to solo unless the Go-Around Procedure is memorized and thoroughly performed to proficiency. The Go-Around Procedure should be introduced on Day-One and continually reviewed on every flight.

The order of the Go-Around Procedure is very important. Note that after the climb attitude is set, a **takeoff-flap setting** must be selected

before raising the landing gear. Why? Because there is much more drag occurring in the full-flap landing configuration than with gear. Moreover, keep in mind that drag does not stop as the gear doors open and close during the retraction process. This is universal on all aircraft.

More importantly, it matters not what positions the throttles, flaps, and landing gear are in, the procedure should be completed by memory, carefully ensuring the correct positioning of each element of the Go-Around Procedure regardless of previous lever positions.

Chapter 7
Basic Instruments (BI) Two Elements: Roll and Pitch

> BI Flying is the foundation for everything else pilots will do while flying in Instrument Flight Rules (IFR). The primary job of a pilot, or autopilot, for that matter, is to set an Attitude. BI Procedures help to accomplish this goal.

Attitudes encompass the Four Fundamentals of Flight: Straight and Level, Turns, Climbs, and Descents. Every maneuver performed in an aircraft incorporates one or more of the Four Fundamentals. This is the primary reason they are called "fundamental."

Knowing how to perform these fundamentals in only Visual Meteorological Conditions (VMC) is no longer acceptable to the FAA for beginning private pilots; it is now imperative that student pilots have a solid grasp of BI.

This is due to the greater demands inherent in our modern ATC system as well as the need to navigate safely and competently during adverse weather conditions. The FAA Practical Flight Exam now expects student pilots to be proficient in BI flying. With Scenario Based Training (SBT), we use visual limiting devices to simulate flying in the clouds, IMC, or night flying with little or no visible horizon.

LEARNING TO FLY - ESSENTIAL ELEMENTS

How is BI flying different from visual flying? If you are thoroughly schooled in attitude flying as discussed earlier in this manual, i.e., knowing all four fundamental procedures and how they relate directly from the top of the glareshield to the visual horizon, the BI procedures are exactly the same with a few important flight limitations.

The key to good BI flying is to know which gauges to monitor on the instrument panel and to understand what those gauges are telling you.

BI is broken down into two elements: Roll and Pitch. These two elements are referenced on the ADI.

I Will First Address Roll

A normal turn in any aircraft—jets or light aircraft—in VMC conditions utilizes 30 degrees of bank. In IMC conditions, or at night, a Standard Rate Turn is utilized. So, how do we calculate a Standard Rate Turn?

Example: Take approach speed of 100 kts, erase the last zero, 10, and add five: (10 + 5) = 15 degrees of bank for a Standard Rate Turn, which is three degrees per second. With jets, having an approach of 200 kts, erase the last zero, 20, and add five: (20 +5) = 25 degrees of bank for a Standard Rate Turn. Thus, *Flight Directors generally limit banks to 25 degrees in jets.

Now that we know how to calculate a Standard Rate Turn, let's establish a limitation for light aircraft drivers and jet aircraft drivers that make it safer to fly in the clouds or at night.

When making any turn in a light aircraft, always limit the bank angle to a maximum of 15 degrees when flying IMC or at night.

---

* **Flight Director:** a flight instrument that is overlaid on the Attitude Indicator that shows the pilot the attitude required to execute the desired flight path.

Basic Instruments (BI) Two Elements: Roll and Pitch

A Jet requires 30 degrees (25 degrees with a Flight Director) because of a higher approach speed and greater turn radius. Jets are also a much more stable instrument platform as opposed to light aircraft, lending them to a greater ease of execution.

In a light aircraft, it is imperative that you establish in your mind a 15-degree bank limitation. Spatial Disorientation (SD) can easily occur. Being aware of this limitation will increase your confidence level while flying in instrument or night conditions.

We've established the max bank angle. Now, how much bank do we require during all flight regimes?

Here is another great gouge (critical tip) that will provide you confidence in knowing how to keep from getting disoriented: always match the degrees of bank with the desired number of degrees of heading-change, not to exceed fifteen degrees at night or in IMC Conditions. Rolling into 15 degrees of bank for a five-degree turn is unproductive and is fertile ground for SD.

Example: If you are assigned a five-degree heading-change, roll into five degrees of bank and wait until the aircraft has turned, then roll out.

A two-degree heading-change would allow for two degrees of bank. Any turn of more than 15 degrees would be limited to a 15-degree bank. Concentrating on this procedure while looking at the ADI will improve your confidence.

I also use this procedure in VFR Daytime Conditions, except allowing for a maximum of 30 degrees of bank. So, if I need to turn 25 degrees to the left, I will use 25 degrees of bank in the turn. Likewise, if I need a 15-degree turn to the right, I'll use 15 degrees of bank. These procedures manifest themselves in smoothness of execution and confidence in knowing what you are doing.

Rolling out of the turn also has a gouge: you should begin your rollout from a turn referencing one-third of your bank. For example, if you are using 15 degrees of bank in this turn, begin your rollout five degrees before your desired heading. Obviously, a two-degree heading-change would not amount to much and would not necessarily be applicable here. Timing of the rollout is important; and with practice, using these gouges will improve your smoothness and technique.

A thorough knowledge of the ADI markings to include the Artificial Horizon, Roll Scale (bank-angle lines), and *Sky Pointer are critical in order to perform these procedures. Familiarize yourself with these terms and know how to use them. I've known experienced pilots who weren't even aware of the Sky Pointer during their entire career.

ADI with Markings

Labels: Roll Scale, Sky Pointer, Roll Pointer, Pitch Scale Markers, Sky, Aircraft Symbol, Ground

The Second Element to BI is Pitch

Because the outside horizon is no longer available to us while in the clouds or at night, we are required to use our ADI to establish our pitch attitudes as well as our bank attitudes. There are three attitudes, or

---

* The **Sky Pointer** is the white triangle in the middle of the bank indicator hash marks at the top of the ADI, developed to aid unusual attitude recovery because it always points to the sky.

Basic Instruments (BI) Two Elements: Roll and Pitch

positions, on the ADI that directly correspond with the outside visual horizon and the glareshield: Climb, Level, and Descent.

There are actually five or six attitudes depending on your type of aircraft and number of flap settings in the descent profile: clean, one-third flaps, two-thirds flaps, and full flaps.

Knowing where to place the tiny center dot (aircraft symbol) for each attitude is necessary to establish the desired maneuver. This can be fine-tuned by noting each pitch while flying in VMC conditions. They can be generally defined as follows:

- Takeoff: 13/15 degrees
- Normal Climb: 7/10 degrees
- Straight and Level: 2/5 degrees
- Descent Clean: -2.5/-1 degrees
- Descent, one-half flaps: -2.5 degrees
- Full Flaps: -3 degrees
- Go-Around: 7/10 degrees

You should calibrate these pitches in your aircraft while flying in VMC conditions and know them well. But, it's not enough to just know your attitudes on the ADI. You must also know how to make corrections after established on a particular attitude; however, it is imperative you make only half-ball corrections in pitch on the ADI.

So, what are half-ball corrections? Remember the tiny dot in the center of the ADI that represents the aircraft? You must create a mindset where the tiny dot becomes a large basketball. Really focusing on this tiny dot and making half-ball corrections are easier to accomplish if you enlarge the dot in your mind.

Now, since we spend 90 percent of our time with only one of the three attitudes, that being Straight and Level, knowing where to look while making those half-ball corrections is imperative to successfully fly good BI. I haven't mentioned power settings other than to say, knowing and utilizing normal visual flight power settings for each fundamental of flight: climbs, level flight, or descents easily corresponds with instrument flying.

Where to look? This is the great conundrum for beginning student pilots. First, we must establish that the ADI is the preeminent focus for most of the time. Note that the ADI is not considered a primary instrument among the six-pack of instruments about which we famously talk. The FAA does not consider it to be an instrument as reflected on the Instrument Rating Written Exam.

Example: If a question on a FAA test asks you to select the primary instruments for level flight, any answer in the multiple-choice list that includes the ADI, which is usually three out of four, is not correct.

This also applies to **Pitch** and **Bank**. Any question asking for the primary instruments for pitch or bank that includes the ADI is the wrong answer. The correct answer does not have the ADI in the answer choice. If the ADI is not an instrument, what is it? Simple, it's outside! It represents what you see out of the window, so start thinking about it in this way. If your flying breaks down while under the hood, concentrate on the ADI, level the wings and establish a stable condition. If you experience SD, the ADI is your life saver.

We know that half-ball corrections in pitch are in order to fly good BI. To do this, we must be able to immediately identify the **Primary Instruments** while performing any of the four fundamentals of flight. These instruments are the same whether you are looking out the window on a clear VMC day or looking on the ADI under the hood.

What is the Primary Instrument for **Level Flight**? The Altimeter. Remember, the ADI is not an instrument. When the Altimeter is moving, is it telling you anything? It's telling you nothing. If you know you are descending or climbing, the Altimeter will be moving in the

Basic Instruments (BI) Two Elements: Roll and Pitch

appropriate direction. You are wasting your time staring at a moving Altimeter. Now, if the Altimeter is not moving, what is it telling you? You are Level.

Takeaway: If your goal is to stay level, taking a peek at the Altimeter and seeing it moving means you need to get your eyes off of it and make an appropriate pitch change on the ADI to stop it from moving. Do not stare at a moving Altimeter. Your eyes should be primarily focused on the ADI to stop the Altimeter from moving.

What is the Primary Instrument for **Pitch**? The Airspeed Indicator. Again, the ADI is not an instrument. When the Airspeed Indicator is moving, is it telling you anything? It's telling you nothing. If you are changing your attitude to the climb, level, or descent position, the Airspeed Indicator will begin to move. You are wasting your time staring at a moving Airspeed Indicator. If you have arrived at and are now stable at the new desired attitude with the appropriate power setting, whether it be climb, level, or descent, the Airspeed Indicator will not be moving. It is the Primary Instrument for Pitch.

Takeaway: Do not stare at a moving Airspeed Indicator. it's telling you nothing. You should be focused on the ADI to establish your desired attitude. Once stabilized at the desired attitude, the Airspeed Indicator confirms your desired pitch attitude.

Finally, what is the Primary Instrument for **Bank**? The DG, your heading indicator just below the ADI. And when the DG is moving, is it telling you anything? It's telling you nothing. If you are expecting it to move because you are turning, staring at it is a waste of time. Now, when the DG is not moving, what is it telling you? You have zero bank and are maintaining your heading. Thus, it is the Primary Instrument for Bank.

Takeaway: Do not stare at a moving DG. If the DG (heading) is moving, take your eyes off of it. You should be focused on the ADI whether you are turning or maintaining a heading.

The bottom line should be knowing where to look when Straight and Level, Turning, Climbing, or Descending.

A quick glance at the Altimeter for Level Flight, a quick glance at the Airspeed Indicator after establishing a Pitch Attitude, or a quick glance at the DG while maintaining a heading is what is necessary for good instrument-flying control. If any of those primary instruments are moving, you are wasting your time staring at them. *Your primary focus should be the ADI.*

CAVEAT: At no time does BI flying negate the invaluable use of the autopilot. Proficient autopilot control can be your best pathway, especially if you experience the startle effect.

Experienced pilots have succumbed to SD, causing loss of life because they thought the autopilot was on, when, in fact, the autopilot was in the off position or in a degraded mode such as control-wheel steering. Not having the presence of mind to confirm the status of the autopilot via the flight mode annunciator, pilots have resigned their fate or have been totally unaware of their situational awareness with disastrous outcomes. Utilizing **Unusual Attitude Procedures** (ch. 11) and solid **BI** understanding and procedures would have saved the day.

There you have it. Roll, Pitch, and how to correct for the Four Fundamentals of Flight under the hood.

* * *

Basic Instruments (BI) Two Elements: Roll and Pitch

BI Brief

Remember that flying under the hood is no different than flying VMC out of the window. Knowing your procedures on how to Climb an aircraft, Level Off an aircraft, and Descend an aircraft are the same whether in VMC or IMC. Beginning students tend to stare at moving instruments when they begin instrument training or experience SD. When training for instrument flying, or experiencing SD, *you must remember* to ignore the moving instruments and focus on the ADI, wings level and applicable attitude.

I can find examples of experienced airline pilots who have killed themselves and/or hundreds of passengers after experiencing SD simply because they did not know to focus on the ADI, or even why. The ADI is analogous to looking out of the window under VMC conditions. It is easy to become bewildered staring at moving instruments, but moving instruments tell you nothing.

There are other gouges you can learn and apply for Instrument Flying which would apply for the higher instrument rating, but what I have just shared here is relevant for 90 percent of what you need to know.

What I have presented here is **BI**. What remains for the advanced ratings is Radio Instruments (**RI**), encompassing instrument approaches and all that go with it. Without proficient knowledge and skill of BI, pilots may become insecure with RI to the point of erratic performance and SD.

To recap, the FAA now requires that private pilots know BI to mitigate the incident and accident rates caused by inadvertent flights into IMC conditions or flying in night operations. ATC also requires a high standard of precision flying on Radar Vectors while flying in class B and C airspace. BI is invaluable in these types of operations.

Learn and memorize these basic limitations along with all the intricate markings of the ADI and practice these procedures while under the hood. It will bear good fruit.

Chapter 8
Slow Flight and Slips

> Confidence is a major factor in a pilot's life. To a fledgling pilot, few maneuvers provide a level of confidence better than those of Slow Flight and Slips. Both maneuvers are excellent tools for every pilot's "stick and rudder" toolkit.

Slow Flight Training should begin early in a student pilot's training, at least by the second flight. Its importance cannot be understated as it provides many aerodynamic perceptions (bits of information) a pilot needs in order to understand and execute fundamental maneuvers.

There are two types of Slips: Forward Slips and Sideslips.

Forward Slips originated in the early days of aviation when most aircraft lacked wing flaps. This allows the pilot to increase the descent rate or to quickly lose altitude without gaining airspeed.

Sideslips have always been around to help pilots easily correct for aircraft and runway alignment.

LEARNING TO FLY - ESSENTIAL ELEMENTS

8.1 Slow Flight

Slow Flight is the pilot's first exposure in flying at the edge of the envelope. This maneuver is a natural progression after mastery of the Four Fundamentals of Flight.

Slow Flight

- Low airspeed
- High angle of attack
- High power setting
- Constant altitude

Vs – Clean

- Perform Two Clearing Turns (Day-One Turn)
- Mixture Rich, Fuel Pump On
- Carb Heat On, Power 1500 RPM, Landing Gear Down
- Maintain Altitude (altimeter does not move) Trimming to Bottom of the Green Arc. Do Not Descend
- **GUMPS**, Landing Checklist Complete
- At First Indication of a Stall, Increase Power to 2000 RPM
- Stabilize Airspeed at Bottom of the Green Arc while Maintaining Altitude. Do Not Allow the Stall Warning Horn to Sound
- If Executing a Turn, Add Power as Necessary to Maintain Flying Speed. Do Not Use More Than 10 Degrees of Bank
- To Recover, Use a Normal **Go-Around Procedure**, Except Transition to Level Flight and Attitude (do not climb), Returning to Normal Cruise. Select an Altitude that will Allow the Task to be Completed No Lower than 1500 feet Above **Ground Level (AGL)**
- Once the **Go-Around Procedure** is Completed and You Are Ready for Normal-Cruise Flight, Complete the **Level-Off Procedure**

Slow Flight and Slips

Vso – Landing Configuration

- Perform Two Clearing Turns
- Mixture Rich, Fuel Pump On
- Carb Heat On, Power 1500 RPM
- Maintain Altitude, Trimming to 80 knots. Do Not Descend (altimeter)
- Flaps One, Landing Gear Down
- **GUMPS**, Landing Checklist Complete
- Flaps Two
- Flaps Three, Trimming to Airspeed (bottom of white arc)
- At First Indication of a Stall, Increase Power to Maintain Airspeed and Altitude. Maintain a minimum airspeed. Any farther increase in AOA, increase in load factor, or reduction in power will result in an immediate stall
- Check Airspeed (bottom of white arc) Do Not Allow the Stall Warning Horn to Sound
- If Executing a Turn, Add Power as Necessary to Maintain Flying Speed. Do Not Use More than 10 Degrees of Bank
- To Recover, Use a Normal **Go-Around Procedure**, Except Transition to Level Flight and Attitude (do not climb), Returning to Normal Cruise
- Once the **Go-Around Procedure** is Completed and You Are Ready for Normal Cruise Flight, Complete the **Level-Off Procedure**

Standards

Establish and maintain an airspeed at which any farther increase of AOA, increase in load factor, or reduction of power would result in an immediate stall.

    Altitude ± 100 feet and Airspeed + 10 / - 0
    Heading ± 10° and Bank ± 10°

LEARNING TO FLY - ESSENTIAL ELEMENTS

Slow Flight Brief

Slow Flight requires the pilot to maintain altitude, heading, and airspeed while the aircraft is in a nose-high attitude at a high AOA. The controls will feel much more sluggish and less responsive. Forward visibility will be reduced as the nose attitude will be so much higher than in normal cruise flight. "S" turning may be required to clear the area while executing this task. It may be more difficult to maintain altitude and heading because of the slow airspeed over the wings. Slow Flight, whether clean (with no flaps), or dirty (with flaps), is referred to as the **"Region of Reverse Command."**

In the Region of Normal Command, any increase in airspeed causes total drag to increase. In the Region of Reverse Command, any increase in airspeed causes total drag to decrease. In Slow Flight, the aircraft experiences a great deal of induced drag as opposed to parasite drag, the sum of the two being total drag.

If you want to climb, forward pressure on the stick will be required with full power to sufficiently reduce the AOA in order to begin the climb. Some recommend to lead the level off from a climb by 10 percent of the rate of climb. I recommend to not level off until you get there, or you will never get there. The climb rate is so small, and the pitch change is so slight, there is no need to anticipate the level off by that much. Turning may require more power to maintain your flying speed. Additionally, the use of right rudder will be necessary to maintain a constant heading due to the left turning tendencies (ch. 14) of the aircraft at slow airspeed and high AOA.

If you want to make a **left turn** with coordinated rudder and aileron, you will need to think **less right-rudder pressure** with left aileron. Conversely, a **right turn** will require an increase in **right-rudder pressure** with aileron. A descent will require a slight reduction in power. The pilot should apply slight forward stick to lower the nose one to two degrees. Trim as necessary. Leveling off from a descent, lead the target altitude by 10 percent of the descent rate. The proper use of trim throughout this maneuver is critical and should be approached

Slow Flight and Slips

carefully and not hurried. Slow Flight has many uses. It is an invaluable aid during training, providing the student pilot a great reference in exhibiting how the aircraft will perform in the landing flare. Search and Rescue as well as Sightseeing Excursions are also practical applications for this maneuver.

8.2 Sideslip

The Purpose of a Sideslip is Twofold:

(1) Aircraft Alignment with the Runway Centerline **(Runway Alignment)**, and (2) Longitudinal Aircraft (nose) Alignment with the Centerline **(Aircraft Alignment)**

Execution:

- Landing Configuration
- Remember: Slips should Never Be Performed Unless the Aircraft is in the Landing Configuration, i.e., Gear Down, Approach Speed (with or without flaps) in the Descent Attitude
- Wing Down for Runway Centerline Alignment
- Rudder for Longitudinal Aircraft (nose) Alignment Parallel to the Runway Centerline Stripes

Sideslip

LEARNING TO FLY - ESSENTIAL ELEMENTS

Sideslip Brief

The Sideslip is executed by the pilot to place the aircraft's longitudinal axis precisely on the center of the runway regardless of the wind. The pilot banks the wing with aileron around the longitudinal axis to maneuver the aircraft sideways to stay aligned with the runway **(Runway Centerline Alignment)**.

At the same time, the pilot is yawing the aircraft with rudder around the vertical axis to keep the longitudinal axis of the aircraft parallel with the runway **(Aircraft Nose Alignment)**.

The image on the adjacent page shows the two types of alignment: Runway Alignment and Aircraft (nose) Alignment.

Always think of what is directly out in front of you as the longitudinal axis of the aircraft. Never reference the nose (prop spinner) with the longitudinal axis of the aircraft.

The same idea applies from the right seat. The sight picture is the same from either seat. If your straight-out sight picture has you on the centerline of the taxiway or runway, the right seat will also have the same sight picture.

Very apparent in Crosswind Landings—if your nose is not lined up from the left seat, the right seat will show the same thing.

Notice the **piece of tape** at the top of the glareshield on the adjacent image representing the longitudinal axis. The object of a crosswind landing is to have the tape (longitudinal axis) parallel and preferably on the centerline of the runway. The pilot accomplishes this by continuously making small corrections with aileron and rudder.

It is too often ignored that the **centerline marking** on the runway is the **main and only** reference point the pilot should be using throughout the entire approach, including the Sideslip.

Slow Flight and Slips

Runway Centerline and Aircraft (nose) Alignment

I refer to the aforementioned procedures as **Crosswind Geometry**. Three things must occur to successfully land an aircraft on the runway:

1. The Aircraft's inertia and flight path must be moving in the same direction as the dotted line on the runway.
2. The Aircraft must flare (raise the nose) by transitioning from the descent attitude to the landing attitude.
3. The Aircraft must be **Sideslipped** to the centerline with the longitudinal axis (piece of tape) precisely on and parallel to the dotted line.

Arriving at the runway with an angling approach already increases the difficulty of the landing because the aircraft inertia and flight path are moving in the wrong direction. Now you have to turn the aircraft while you are flaring, and perhaps **Sideslipping**, to maintain the centerline and straightened nose position. Performing all three of the above items exponentially increases the difficulty of the landing maneuver. Mitigating this scenario, the sooner you place your body on the extended centerline and keep it there is one less thing you will have to do at the runway.

If you are on a 10-mile, straight-in approach, immediately turn the aircraft and line up—the sooner the better. Never accept an angling approach. Mentally picture the extended centerline from the runway centerline and put yourself there. All you now have to do is flare and **Sideslip** to your landing.

In a strong crosswind, an early runway alignment can also show you the effects of the wind. You cannot see the wind, but you can see the effects of the wind. I cannot overemphasize the need to stay on the extended runway centerline. Flare at the appropriate time and touch down with the aircraft nose straight and on the centerline.

8.3 Forward Slip

The Purpose of a Forward Slip is to Lose Altitude on an Approach.

Execution:

- Landing Configuration
- Remember: Slips should Never be Performed unless the Aircraft is in the Landing Configuration, I.e., Gear Down, Approach Speed (with or without flaps) in the Descent Attitude
- Full Rudder to the Floor
- Opposite Wing Down

Forward Slip Brief

Forward Slips provide a means to increase the descent rate in order to recapture a proper glideslope for a normal, stabilized descent and landing. It is not a Forward Slip unless the rudder is completely depressed to the floor. As a word of caution, depressing the rudder to the floor will create angular momentum, allowing the nose to rise.

It is imperative while in a bank that you do not allow the nose to rise. Forward pressure on the yoke is essential to maintain the descent attitude. The other way to increase the descent rate is the use of flaps; flaps allow you to fly slower approach speeds.

Slow Flight and Slips

Many aircraft have limitations concerning the use of Forward Slips. Forward Slips may be prohibited on some aircraft with flaps extended beyond the takeoff-flap position. **Reference your POH.** Operation with the flaps fully extended may block the rudder while performing Forward Slips.

There are many other scenarios where Forward Slips may be desired. A loss of flaps control, a symmetry problem with the flaps, or other system abnormals precluding the normal deployment of flaps, coupled with a high glideslope situation, would make the Forward Slip an agreeable alternative.

Aircraft without any flaps, e.g., the Piper Cub, the Aeronica 7AC Champion, and the Luscombe 8A, to name a few, make the Forward Slip a necessary performance skill in a pilot's toolkit.

Remember, Forward Slips are performed only when the aircraft is in a landing configuration on **Final Approach**—on an appropriate approach speed—regardless of the flaps position (clean, one/half, or full flaps). Forward Slips are not used for enroute descents regardless of how high you may find yourself. A 360-degree descending turn would be a more appropriate alternative in this Enroute or Terminal-Approach Scenario."

Chapter 9
Stalls

> A Stall occurs when an aircraft wing stops producing lift due to an excessive Angle of Attack (AOA), that point being the Critical Angle of Attack (C-AOA).

The AOA is the angle between the wing's chord line and the oncoming airflow (see image on page 23). It's not a fixed angle of degrees but a specific condition of airflow relative to the wing.

To recover from a Stall, the AOA must be reduced below the C-AOA. Pilots must train to recognize a Stall and how to recover from it.

There have been numerous situations where pilots did not first reduce the AOA and instead prioritized power and maintaining altitude which resulted in a loss of control.

Careful application of the following procedures should provide the necessary protection from a Stall and loss of control.

As always, a pilot should follow the aircraft-specific manufacturer's recommended procedures (POH) if published and current.

LEARNING TO FLY - ESSENTIAL ELEMENTS

9.1 Approach to Landing Stall-Power Off

- Perform Two Clearing Turns (Day-One Turn)
- Mixture Rich, Fuel Pump On
- Carb Heat On, Power 1500 RPM
- **Maintain Level Altitude, Trimming to 80 Knots. Do Not Descend**
- At 80 Knots, Nose to Descent Attitude
- Flaps as Desired, **Three Scenarios** (landing gear down after first notch of flaps):

  (1) Clean, Landing Gear Down (abeam with zero bank)
  (2) Flaps Two Notches (base turn/20-degree max bank angle)
  (3) Full Flaps (final approach with zero bank)

- **TRIM**
- Landing Checklist **(GUMPS)**
- **Stabilize on Airspeed with the Appropriate Flap Configuration and Descent Attitude**
- Power Idle
- Set Climb Attitude, Increase AOA
- At First Indication of a Stall (C-AOA) (stick-shaker, horn, buffet) Announce **("Stall, Stall, Stall")**
- *****Stick Forward**, Reduce AOA
- **Perform the Go-Around Procedure**

After the Go-Around Procedure is completed, expect to level off using the normal Level-Off Procedure.

---

*   With stick (yoke) forward on recovery, the FAA wants to see a nose-down attitude slightly below the horizon. In the past, it was considered desirable to maintain altitude or even a slight climb on the recovery. Remember, an aircraft can be stalled at any attitude or airspeed and recovered the same way as long as you have reduced the AOA below the C-AOA. Since the accident rate has become considerably higher with these types of events, pilots are now required to adapt to this new procedure.

Stalls

Approach to Landing Stall (Power Off) Brief

To Stall a wing means to put the wing in a position where the air meeting the wing will no longer support the wing. As the wing moves through the air, the angle at which the air meets the wing is called the AOA.

How many Angles of Attack are there? Actually, 180 degrees from the leading edge of the wing continuing below the wing to the trailing edge (positive AOA) and 180 degrees above the wing to the trailing edge (negative AOA).

What causes the wing to Stall? There is only one answer: the wing reaches the C-AOA. At the C-AOA, around 18 degrees positive AOA in most aircraft, the airflow over the wing is disrupted and separates from the wing, causing the wing to no longer fly smoothly through the air. Basically, the wing quits flying as illustrated below:

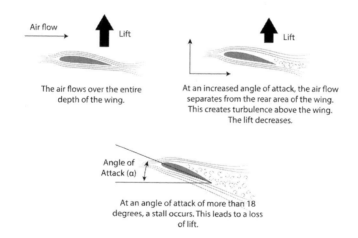

What controls the AOA? Answer: the elevator, stabilator, or whatever you have installed on your aircraft that controls pitch.

The only way to get the wing to start flying again is to reduce the **AOA** below the **C-AOA**. Achieve this by moving the stick or yoke forward. If I perform a loop and reach the top of the loop upside down and suddenly stall the aircraft, which way do I move the elevator control?

Again, stick-forward. The only time it would be stick-aft is if you were doing an outside maneuver. How many times do we perform outside negative-G maneuvers? Unless you are Sean Tucker, or another world-class aerobatic performer, that is not going to happen.

Also remember, an aircraft will Stall at any airspeed or attitude. All that has to be done is to reach the C-AOA. Every month the United States averages around 15 to 20 GA fatal accidents. Many of these accidents involve this very subject: placing the aircraft in a threatening C-AOA situation. Almost every checkride involves a Stall-Maneuver Demonstration to ensure that pilots are educated and proficient in the recovery process. So why do we have such a problem with this?

Mechanics

The mechanics of a Stall and Recovery should be emphasized. How does one recognize that a wing is Stalled? Horn-sound, stick-shaker, or buffeting are standard warning signs against which to guard. At the moment of any of these signs, what must be immediately done? Answer: Stick or Yoke Forward.

If you experience angular momentum (rotation) at this time, you are now in the state of an incipient (beginning stage) spin. Once you are experiencing a Stall or Spin, how do you recognize that you are flying and no longer in a Stalled Condition after an attempted recovery? Only one answer: if the airspeed is *not* accelerating, you have *not* recovered.

You must keep the stick forward. If you prematurely program the stick back to neutral, you will only aggravate the Stall or Spin, leading to a Secondary Stall. You must keep the stick forward until the airspeed begins to increase. Increasing airspeed will allow the wing to fly.

An increase in airspeed accompanied by angular momentum is now the beginning of a Spiral. Then, and only then, you will program the stick aft to recover from the dive. If spinning (airspeed not accelerating), the **ailerons** need to be **neutralized** and only the rudder utilized to stop the rotation of the Spin.

Stalls

We use the acronym PARE to recover from a Spin

    P – Power to Idle
    A – Ailerons Neutral
    R – Rudder Opposite the Turn Needle
    E – Elevators, Stick Forward

Remember, you can Stall an aircraft at any attitude: Climbing, Level, or Descending, so I emphasize stick forward.

Recognizing the dismal accident rate with Stall/Spin Scenarios, the FAA, assuming a checkride scenario of one G with a normal flight attitude, expects pilot applicants on checkrides and flight reviews (after the initial stick forward recovery) to recover from the Stall by placing the attitude of the aircraft in a **slight nose-down attitude** below the horizon. In other words, expect to lose some altitude. Once the wing is flying, then a normal recovery can be made by doing the Go-Around Procedure. See chapter 11 on unusual attitudes to understand recovery from extremely nose-high attitudes.

If the examiner asks you the difference between a Spin and a Spiral, you can now answer that **Airspeed** is the difference.

Angular momentum **without** an increase in speed is a **Spin**. Remember, a Spin is a stalled aircraft with rotation. Angular momentum **with** an increased airspeed is a **Spiral**.

Recovery from a Secondary Stall or a Cross-Control Stall again requires the positive stick forward recovery procedure. Recovering from a Stall too aggressively, or a windshear or wake turbulence event, may induce a Secondary Stall. Cross-Controlling the aircraft as in a Slip or a Skid with an increase in AOA to the C-AOA will produce the same stalling result. Without an immediate Stall Recovery, the aircraft is susceptible to inducing angular momentum rolling into a Spin and will begin to roll opposite the position of the ball on the *inclinometer.

Aeronautical Decision Making (ADM)

Now that I have reviewed the mechanics of a Stall/Spin State, the other aspect about Stalls is what scenarios you should think about when practicing for a checkride. Again, the FAA emphasizes **ADM** as a process to mitigate the Stall/Spin accident rate. What does that mean? You should be asking yourself from where the threats come?

Looking at where those accidents largely occur, the FAA utilizes SBT to reinforce what the pilot should think about as Stalls are performed. Since most of the Stall/Spin accidents occur when an aircraft is closest to the ground, the Traffic Pattern is the most logical place to look.

There are Three Scenarios for Approach to Landing Stalls:

1. Simulating the aircraft on approach just **abeam** of the touchdown point of the runway. Obviously, you would want to practice these maneuvers at or above the required altitude of 1500 feet for single-engine aircraft, or at or above 3000 feet for multi-engine aircraft. Remember, any part of the maneuver cannot go below these altitudes.

2. Simulating the aircraft in a **turn on base to final approach** with the appropriate flap configuration.

3. The aircraft **fully configured on final approach** to land.

These three scenarios are carefully notated on the Approach to Landing Stall (power off) procedure checklist (sec. 9.1). Once configured and

---

* **The Inclinometer,** also known as the "ball in a tube," is used to indicate coordinated flight. Located below the "rate of turn" indicator, it is a black ball suspended in a liquid that allows it to roll right, left, or remain in the middle, depending on the aircraft's slip/skid (balance) condition.

Stalls

on speed for each scenario in the appropriate attitude, all that is required to complete the task is to:

- Bring the power to complete idle
- Increase the AOA (elevator) to the C-AOA (climb attitude)
- Announce **"Stall, Stall, Stall"**
- Stick Forward (nose slightly below the horizon)
- Perform the Go-Around Procedure

9.2 Takeoff/Departure Stalls-Power On

- Perform Two Clearing Turns (Day-One Turn)
- Place Aircraft in Takeoff Condition: Mixture-Rich, Fuel Pump On, Carb Heat On, Power 1500 RPM, Trim Set to Takeoff Position
- Slow to Takeoff Speed
- Maintain **Level** Attitude and Altitude while Trimming. **Do Not Descend**
- Clean or Takeoff Flaps as Desired (landing gear down after first notch of flaps)
- Landing Checklist **(GUMPS)**
- Stabilize the Aircraft on Airspeed and Altitude at the Bottom of the Green Arc with the Appropriate Flaps Setting (clean or takeoff-flap setting)
- Nose to the Climb Attitude (increase AOA)
- Full Power, Carb Heat Off
- **For Takeoff Stall:** Wings Level and Clean
- **For Departure Stall:** Commence a Turn with No More than 20 Degrees of Bank Angle
- At First Indication of a Stall (C-AOA) (stick-shaker, horn, buffet) Announce **"Stall, Stall, Stall"**
- **Stick Forward** (nose slightly below the horizon), Reduce AOA, **Level Wings**
- **Perform the Go-Around Procedure.** (continued on next page)

LEARNING TO FLY - ESSENTIAL ELEMENTS

After the Go-Around Procedure is completed, expect to level off using the normal Level-Off Procedure.

Takeoff / Departure Stalls (Power On) Brief

Assume you are taking off from a runway (the point of **liftoff** from the runway) for a **takeoff scenario**, or departing the traffic pattern after airborne for a **departure scenario**. Place the aircraft in either one of these two conditions before commencing the Stall Maneuver.

After completing your two Clearing Turns (Day-One Turn), you want to stabilize the aircraft in level flight, placing the aircraft just as it would be at liftoff (scenario number one). Reduce speed to the bottom of the green arc but not below the Stall Speed, trim wheel in the takeoff position, and the landing gear down with flaps in the takeoff setting. Stabilize the aircraft at that speed and configuration with power. You are now ready to begin the maneuver. Your aircraft may or may not require flaps for takeoff. **I usually perform the Takeoff Stall with zero flaps and the Departure Stall with takeoff flaps set.**

Never begin to increase the attitude until you are completely stabilized. The altimeter should not be moving. Now it's just a matter of placing the throttle where it would normally be in a real takeoff situation. Increase power while raising the nose to the Climb Attitude. Set the attitude without trimming and keep it there. As the aircraft slows, be patient, keeping the ball centered with coordinated flight (right rudder).

Once you have experienced one of the warning signs of an approaching C-AOA, announce "Stall, Stall, Stall" as you are programing the stick or yoke forward. After recovering from the Stall, immediately perform a Go-Around Procedure. After the Go-Around Procedure is completed, expect to level off using the normal level-off procedure.

The Departure Stall utilizes the same entry procedures except, once stabilized in the climb, roll into a turn not exceeding **20 degrees of bank with a takeoff-flap setting**. Carefully note the ball and the use of rudder while making a coordinated turn.

Stalls

Everything else is the same, maintaining the Climb Attitude with power on and waiting until the aircraft begins the symptoms of a stalled wing. At the Stall, stick forward as you are announcing **"Stall, Stall, Stall,"** level the wings, and recover with a Go-Around Procedure.

9.3 Accelerated Stall

- Perform Two Clearing Turns. (Day-One Turn)
- Mixture Rich, Fuel Pump On
- Carb Heat On, Power 1500 RPM, Landing Gear Down
- Maintain LEVEL Altitude (altimeter does not move)
- **TRIM**
- At 80 Knots, Nose to the **Clean Descent Attitude** and Stabilize

    Slow to 1.3 times Vs Speed (airspeed must never exceed Va maneuver speed for this task)

- Roll Into a 45-degree Bank Angle (simulates base to final turn)
- Reduce Power to Idle and Smoothly Increase Back Elevator Pressure , Increase AOA
- At First Indication of a Stall (C-AOA) (stick-shaker, horn, buffet) Announce **"Stall, Stall, Stall"**
- **Stick Forward**, Reduce AOA
- Perform the **Go-Around Procedure** while Rolling **Wings Level**

After the Go-Around Procedure is completed, expect to level off using the normal Level-Off Procedure.

Accelerated Stall Brief

The purpose of an Accelerated Stall is to demonstrate that an aircraft can be Stalled at any airspeed and attitude provided the C-AOA is attained. It is imperative that a prolonged stall, excessive airspeed, excessive loss of altitude, or a spin be avoided.

LEARNING TO FLY - ESSENTIAL ELEMENTS

This maneuver is important for how it begins, with the aircraft's attitude in the Descent-Attitude Position. Seeing this nose-down sight picture may cause the pilot to become complacent as this attitude usually occurs at a low AOA. It appears non-threatening and safe; however, putting an excessive elevator back pressure G load on the aircraft with a 45-degree bank, even with the nose in a seemingly safe descent attitude, will nevertheless cause the aircraft to Stall.

This scenario is, unfortunately, all too common in GA as reflected in the high accident rate. Anytime you see that you are going to overshoot your "Turn-to-Final" or whatever you are trying to accomplish, you need to level the wings and Go-Around.

Putting an additional load on the aircraft knows no bounds as far as the attitude of the aircraft is concerned. The attitude will not save you unless the wing is unloaded:

Stick-forward, unload the wing, and do a Go-Around.

We begin this maneuver by doing two Clearing Turns and initially putting the aircraft in the landing condition. Slow to Vs x 1.3 speed, landing gear down with no flaps. The goal is to **stabilize** the aircraft at this clean speed in the Descent Attitude. This should easily comply with the airspeed below Va maneuver speed. Flaps should not be extended because the of risk of exceeding the maximum flaps extended speed in the Stall Recovery. Once stabilized in the clean, descent attitude, roll into 45 degrees of bank and begin a pull on the stick/yoke (elevator). Continue the pull with enough positive G pressure, not allowing the aircraft to descend until the aircraft begins the signs of a Stall (stick-shaker, horn, or buffet). Pulling the aircraft at the Level Flight Attitude (altimeter not moving) should mitigate any tendency to spiral downward, which can be just as careless as stalling the aircraft, especially turning base to final low to the ground.

The recovery is straightforward: unload the wing (stick forward) while announcing **"Stall, Stall, Stall,"** rolling the wings level with coordinated rudder and aileron, while performing the **Go-Around**

Stalls

Procedure. The G load will not hurt the aircraft as long as you are below Va maneuver speed.

Referring to the chart below, you can see that an aircraft bank over 83 degrees cannot allow the wings to fly. Sixty degrees of bank in a level turn equates to a load factor of two Gs, twice the weight of the aircraft and souls onboard.

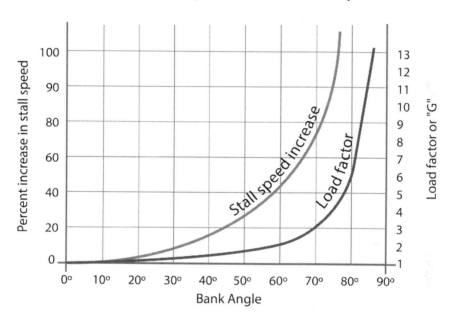

Stall Speed Compared to Load Factor Graph

Notice that the load factor increases exponentially beyond 60 degrees of bank while trying to stay on altitude.

Remember that FAA regulations require the use of a parachute when performing maneuvers of over 60 degrees of bank.

Chapter 10
Steep Turns

> Steep Turns remain within a pilot's career and are included in most Flight Checks regardless of what pipeline is pursued, be it civilian, military, charter, airline, or others.

We practice performance maneuvers like Steep Turns not only because they are a required maneuver on flight checks but also because they have many practical uses. They prepare a pilot for emergencies like collision avoidance; they develop a pilot's skill in hand-eye coordination, SA, and aircraft coordination; they teach a pilot to efficiently divide his/her attention between the inside and outside of the aircraft. And they are fun! One AOPA writer describes the Steep Turn as an "officially sanctioned moment of fighter pilot fantasy."

Mastering the Steep Turn, along with other performance maneuvers, will increase smoothness in your flight-control application, increase your ability to sense the aircraft's attitude and orientation, and prepare you to perform more advanced flight maneuvers. For Sport and Private Pilots, ACS standards for the number of Steep Turns leave it up to the examiner; however, commercial pilot and flight instructor certification require two 360-degree turns in opposite directions.

LEARNING TO FLY - ESSENTIAL ELEMENTS

Steep Turn

- Perform Two Clearing Turns (Day-One Turn), Reference a Prominent Landmark
- Stabilize the Aircraft on Altitude and a Cardinal Heading (N.E.S.W.)
- Slow to Below Maneuvering Speed **(Va)**
- Bank into the Turn (45 degrees Private, 50 degrees Commercial)
- Add Power **(to maintain airspeed)**, Do not Trim
- Maintain Level Flight (altimeter does not move), Elevator Back Pressure to Maintain a Level Sight Picture. Scan Bank, Nose Attitude, and Altimeter (continuously)
- Turn 360 Degrees and Begin Your Rollout (landmark). Begin Rollout Heading within One-Half of the Bank, Forward Pressure as You Roll Immediately into the Other Direction
- Continue in the Other Direction, Maintaining Altitude. Scan Bank, Nose Attitude, and Altimeter (continuously)
- After 360 Degrees Turn, Roll Out on Your Landmark, Elevator Forward Pressure, Reduce Power

Steep Turn

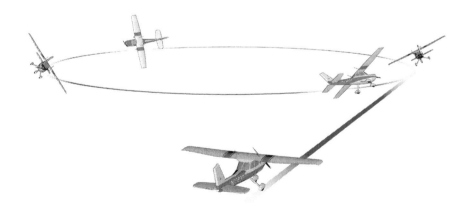

Steep Turns

Steep Turns Brief

Regardless of the pilot's experience level, proficiency in Steep Turns has always been an important requisite in a pilot's toolkit. A rookie pilot's introductory sensation in a Steep Turn is the feeling of heaviness in the seat during the 45-degree bank turn. In aviation parlance, we address this as G loading, also expressed as acceleration. G loading, or acceleration, is not just referring to speed; any change in direction is also acceleration regardless of the speed.

There are three elements of acceleration in pilot parlance: Positive G, Negative G, and Transverse G.

- **Positive G** acceleration (steep turn) forces the blood in your body to flow away from your head to your feet.
- **Negative G** (outside aerobatic maneuvers) forces the blood upward toward your head.
- **Transverse G** (lying flat on your back as an astronaut would experience in a rocket launch) forces the blood from the front of the body to the back.

The body can sustain many more Transverse Gs than Positive or Negative Gs. This is why astronauts are required to lie on their backs to withstand the tremendous "acceleration G forces" on the body during their launch. Excessive Positive G over time can produce a black-out. Excessive Negative G over time can produce a red-out.

One G is the weight experienced as one stands, sits, or lies down at rest. We label this as a **load factor** of one. As you roll into a bank in an aircraft, you begin to change direction, which creates acceleration (G loading). For every given bank angle in level flight at a constant speed, there is a **constant load factor** (page 85).

Multiplying the load factor with the weight of the aircraft, or the weight of your body, will provide the actual force in pounds supported by the wings of the aircraft, or the force of your body pressing down into the seat.

A normal 30-degree, medium-bank level turn gives you a 1.154 load factor. Sixty degrees of bank gives you a load factor of 2. A Steep Turn with a 45-degree bank (Private Pilot requirement) gives you a 1.414 load factor. A Steep Turn with a 50-degree bank (Commercial Pilot requirement) gives you a 1.5 load factor.

I mention all this to assure that you will not be subjected to an unreasonable G force. With a Private Pilot 45-degree bank requirement, the load factor is only 1.414. Multiplying 1.414 by your weight will give you a number you should be able to deal with as you become proficient with the maneuver. The weight pressing into your seat is easily tolerable and quickly adaptable. Banking the aircraft at 60 degrees will have you experience your weight times two. A bank over 60 degrees is prohibited unless you are wearing a parachute. We do not carry parachutes for normal flight training.

A **Steep-Turn Scan** requires three basic elements:

Bank (Attitude Indicator)
Pitch Attitude (Glareshield VMC or Attitude Indicator IMC)
Level Flight (Altimeter)

Level Flight means to not let the altimeter move. If it is moving it is telling you nothing. If you see movement during a glance, immediately focus outside and make a pitch change (VMC) to stop it from moving. Once the altimeter is stopped, it is telling you that you are in level flight. Never stare at a moving instrument. Again, the ADI is not considered an instrument.

As you roll into the 45-degree bank, you want to focus on the attitude (outside), and the bank. The bank is indicated on the Attitude Gyro in front of you. Beginning with your first **Steep Turn**, you should try to memorize the bank angle while looking outside and referencing the horizon, so as not to scan the ADI so much.

Some aircraft have a tendency to **overbank** while in the turn. This is caused by several reasons and is different for various aircraft. As long

Steep Turns

as you are in coordinated flight with the inclinometer ball centered, it is okay to use the ailerons to maintain your desired bank. If the ailerons are not neutral, the aircraft is not in a cross-control situation with which you need to be concerned. You are merely maintaining your bank as long as you are in coordinated flight.

An **overbank** scenario coupled with an increase in G loading (an increase in back pressure on the yoke) may result in an Accelerated Stall. A decrease in bank below 45 degrees to re-establish the turn will prevent the threat of an Accelerated Stall.

One last item: when an examiner asks you why we add power in a Steep Turn, there is only one answer: **to Maintain Airspeed**. I rarely get the right answer when I pose this question to pilots of all types. One of my students owns and operates an 18-wheel tractor trailer. I asked him what happens to the truck when he approaches a large hill and he doesn't add power? It slows down. You must add power to maintain your speed. A Steep Turn, rolling 45 degrees, is like a truck climbing a steep hill—hopefully, not 45 degrees, but same analogy. You are placing the 45-degree hill on its side. Voila; a Steep Turn!

In all the jets I have flown, the application of power has always been an addition of eight percent N1 (power gauge). In light aircraft, full power is needed. In HP-piston aircraft, the power must be determined by the pilot—whatever it takes to maintain your entry speed—which should be below **maneuver speed (Va)**. During the Steep Turn you must maintain plus or minus 10 knots. So, remember to add power to **maintain airspeed**.

> Do not add power to maintain altitude. Altitude is maintained with pitch referencing the altimeter. You must not let the altimeter move. Airspeed and Altitude are two very important distinctions in a Steep Turn. Pilots must know and understand these distinctions well.

Chapter 11
Unusual (Critical) Attitudes

> An aircraft may enter an Unusual Attitude when an "Upset Event" occurs such as wake turbulence, pitch up greater than 25 degrees, pitch down greater that 10 degrees, bank angle greater than 45 degrees, or flying with insufficient airspeed within these zones.

Unusual Attitudes imply that the pilot becomes distracted with something else while flying, only to find the aircraft is not in the position that the pilot expected, whether it be straight and level, a turn, a climb, or a descent.

This scenario has led to the deaths of hundreds of people when even seasoned pilots have become startled and experienced SD. Pilots must remain vigilant, guarding against this occurrence.

Reliance on automation and the autopilot can exacerbate this phenomenon. Subsequently, BI goes out the window because the pilot's mindset, for whatever reason, does not allow him/her to focus on the ADI. All pilots train for these "Upset Events" in flight schools as well as with private instructors.

LEARNING TO FLY - ESSENTIAL ELEMENTS

Here is a five-step procedure to provide proficiency for pilots to combat SD and that surprised, startled event:

Step One: Disconnect

Do not assume anything. **Disconnect the autopilot while focusing on the ADI.** It matters not whether you believe it is on or off. Push the autopilot disconnect button *twice:* once to disconnect and once for the spouse and kids. When you have completed all five steps, you will have plenty of time to reconcile the autopilot requirements.

Step Two: Assess

Assess the pitch attitude of the aircraft. There are only three of them: nose-**high**, nose-**level**, nose-**low**.

Step Three: Power

If the nose is above the horizon, **add power**. If the nose is below the horizon, **reduce power**. If the nose is level, power adjustment is not necessary.

Step Four: Roll

If the nose is high, **roll away** from the Sky Pointer.

The objective is to lower the nose toward the horizon in order to improve your recovery attitude. Many flight schools teach that out of a nose-high attitude you must lower the nose with forward pressure on the elevator control. However, the use of coordinated aileron and rudder, coupled with zero G elevator control (unloading the wing), rolling away from the Sky Pointer, is the better procedure. This is taught by the military, the airlines, and all the business simulator training companies. A high AOA attitude with little or no elevator effectiveness—regardless of aircraft type and the threat of compressor stalls in jets—justifies never pushing down on the elevator control.

The higher the initial nose attitude, more rudder and less aileron is required. The controversy is not getting the nose down, but *how* to get the nose down. The acceptable procedure is to put the aircraft on its

Unusual (Critical) Attitudes

side, banking to the right or left away from the Sky Pointer, depending on how you initially found the aircraft position.

Rolling more than 30 degrees is not necessary, unless you find yourself already in a greater bank or an extremely nose-high attitude. In that case, just let the nose fall with coordinated rudder and aileron. You **roll away** from the Sky Pointer, looking for the horizon on the **ADI**. At that point, you **roll out** of the bank.

Remember, the higher the nose, the less aileron is required and the more rudder is required. If you are looking straight up, vertically, it's all rudder and a little opposite aileron to keep from rolling on your back. Of course, this scenario (actually called a hammerhead stall) will quickly require you to bring your power to idle since you will subsequently be heading straight down.

With power off, all that's left to do is level the wings, rolling to the Sky Pointer and pulling out of the dive. You do not want the power on at this time while heading straight down. It would be *disastrous*.

If the nose is low, **roll to** the Sky Pointer.

Step Five: Pull

Once the wings are level, **pull** to the level pitch attitude. Remember, this is where BI procedures come into play. Really focus on that **ADI**.

* * *

Memorize These Procedures used by the Military, the Airlines, and all the Business Simulator Training Companies:

- **Disconnect** (the autopilot)
- **Assess** (nose high or low)
- **Power** + or − (nose high = add, nose low = reduce)
- **Roll** (high: roll **away**, low: roll **to**) the Sky Pointer
- **Pull** (out of the dive)

Chapter 12
Tracking (Crab)

> A Crab uses a coordinated turn to position the aircraft heading to correct for Wind Drift. This maneuver allows the aircraft to track a straight-line course across the ground.

In aviation lingo, "Crab" means to fly an aircraft with the nose facing into a crosswind to compensate for drift. The aircraft will resemble a crab scuttling sideways across the sand. The Crab may be used in all phases of flight, including flight cruising at top altitude. Jets experiencing high-velocity jet streams exceeding 100 knots may have to Crab a fair amount of degrees into the crosswind to maintain a straight, constant ground track.

Crabbing is especially important during Final to the runway to prevent an angling approach. From the time you observe the dotted line of the runway, make every effort to place the extended centerline under the seat of your aircraft.

The Crab is here your friend. Avoid angling approaches like the plague. Once in close to the runway, the Sideslip—wing down, top rudder—is your tool to make the landing.

LEARNING TO FLY - ESSENTIAL ELEMENTS

Execution:

- Determine your track by picking two points directly in line in front of you and watch for movement.
- Determine the direction of Wind Drift.
- Perform a coordinated turn into the wind, and stop your turn on a heading you estimate will stop the wind drift.
- Once this Crab-Angle is established, maintain watch on both points to maintain your straight-line track.
- Keep the wings level while the nose is aligned with the wind and the flight path is centered.
- Before touching down, transition from a Crab to a Sideslip to land successfully.

The Tracking (Crab) Method Approach

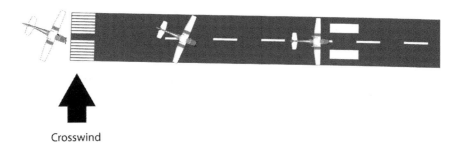

Crosswind

At no time during this maneuver should you apply uncoordinated controls (slipping or skidding) until you begin the transition to the Sideslip for landing.

Tracking Crab Brief

Because of the wind, it's necessary to understand how your aircraft is affected. Headwinds, Tailwinds, and Crosswinds may get you to your destination quicker, slower, or not at all. More than one student pilot has become lost because Wind Drift was never compensated for, or it was incorrectly applied, during the flight planning prep. Careful

Tracking (Crab)

preflight planning with your flight instructor during the cross-country phase, learning how to use pilotage, dead reckoning, and radio navigation, along with the knowledge to correct for wind, are very necessary in today's airspace.

While maneuvering in the traffic pattern, knowledge of how to fly an accurate ground track is essential. The Day-One Turn addresses the importance of picking a point before you turn so as to be able to roll out of the turn, tracking to the point.

Pilots should divide their time 70 percent outside and 30 percent inside the aircraft.

They should also strive to focus outside the aircraft to verify bank angle and pitch. Looking straight out at the horizon, visualizing the attitude of the aircraft—climb, level, or descent—should be automatic. Rolling into a coordinated turn, carefully using your rudder to keep the nose cowling stationary without having to look inside at the inclinometer, is also a skill you should master.

Looking outside at the ground to determine the Wind Drift in reference to points on the ground should also become automatic in your flying skills. Now, it should be evident why you must look outside the aircraft 70 percent of the time. You will have plenty of time to verify heading, bank, and altitude during the 30 percent you are inside the aircraft.

Takeaway: Continually practice picking points—using your horizon and visual cues such as bank, nose position, and attitude during all phases of flight—and hone these skills until they become automatic.

And again, do everything the same way every time and it will not take 500 hours of flight time to become a proficient pilot.

Chapter 13
Ground Reference Maneuvers

> Ground Reference Maneuvers combine the four fundamentals of fight (straight and level, turns, climbs, and descents) into cohesive skills a pilot uses in everyday flight activity.

Ground Reference Maneuvers teach students to utilize their senses of sight, sound, and touch while developing "division of attention" skills to accurately place the aircraft in relationship to specific references while maintaining a desired ground track.

Since the wind influences your ground track, pilots must first be familiar with the effects of Wind Drift to effectively perform these maneuvers. The goal is to safely maneuver the aircraft while flying at low altitude, making corrections for the wind. You can't see the wind, but you can see its effects on your aircraft. You should have a general idea of wind direction before you take off.

Aviation weather reports provide wind direction, as do airport wind socks. Once airborne, steam and smoke stacks offer clues, and windmills always point in the direction from where the wind is coming. Sometimes there is no wind, eliminating the need for any correction.

LEARNING TO FLY - ESSENTIAL ELEMENTS

Most important is to fly coordinated, limit your bank, and remain cognizant of any other traffic.

The student pilot is responsible to know three specific Ground Reference Maneuvers, any of which the examiner may select for the Private Pilot Flight Examination:

- Rectangular Course
- S-Turns Across a Road
- Turns About a Point

13.1 Rectangular Course

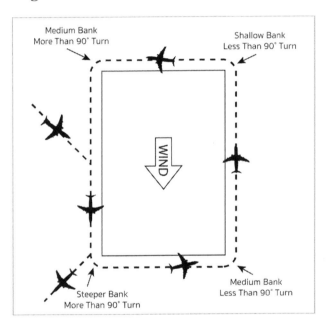

The Rectangular Course is really learning how to track (Crab) a line and make constant-radius turns while understanding and compensating for the effects of the wind. The Rectangular Course entry expects the applicant to enter the 45-degree line to the downwind much like a traffic pattern. Keep in mind that it is standard practice to enter Ground Reference Maneuvers downwind where groundspeed is the greatest.

Ground Reference Maneuvers

Perform your turns around your checkpoints in the Rectangular Course with constant-radius turns compensating for the wind. Turning into a headwind, the bank will vary on the low side, starting with a shallow bank. Conversely, turning into a tailwind, a greater bank will have to be initiated to provide you with that constant-radius turn.

13.2 S-Turns Across a Road

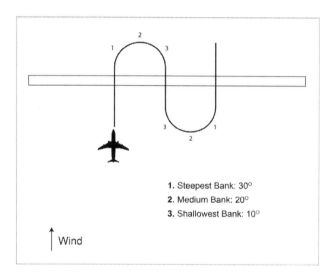

1. Steepest Bank: 30°
2. Medium Bank: 20°
3. Shallowest Bank: 10°

S-Turns Across a Road provide an exercise in correcting for the wind through the application of Roll Rate, Bank Angle, and Wind-Correction Angle:

At point 1: because the ground speed is the fastest, apply a rapid but not aggressive roll rate to 30 degrees of max bank angle.

At point 2: the turn should be more than 90 degrees, Crabbing into the wind. This is your wind-correction angle. Apply a medium bank angle of 20 degrees with corresponding slower roll rates.

LEARNING TO FLY - ESSENTIAL ELEMENTS

At point 3: a shallow, 10-degree bank is applied. Keep in mind that the roll rate should vary throughout the maneuver: a faster rate with a faster groundspeed, a slower rate with a slower groundspeed, etc., playing the turn to arrive over the road and perpendicular to the road.

13.3 Turns About a Point

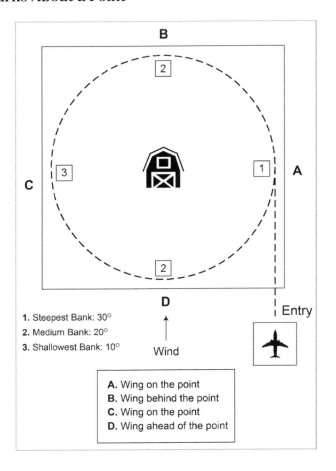

Turns About (or Around) a Point are 360-degree constant-radius turns around a single ground-based reference point. Again, standard practice is to enter downwind where the fastest groundspeed occurs.

Ground Reference Maneuvers

At point A: apply a max bank angle of 30 degrees, a rapid but not aggressive roll rate, turning more than 90 degrees by **point B** for a wind-correction angle (wing behind the point).

A continuous turn, utilizing lesser bank angles and roll rates as the groundspeed decreases, through **points C and D,** allows the aircraft to maintain a constant-radius turn.

Point D requires a Crab (your wind-correction angle), into the wind with the wing ahead of the point.

I have included Eights Across a Road and Eights Along a Road in this section to aid in your understanding of the effects of the wind.

13.4 Eights Across a Road

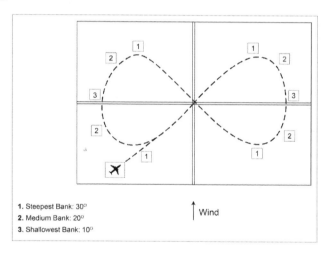

Eights Across a Road involve the same principles and techniques as the other Ground Reference Maneuvers: Bank Angle, Roll Rate, and Wind Correction Angle.

At the completion of each loop of the Figure Eight, the airplane should cross an intersection or a specific ground reference point.

The depicted loops should be across the road, and the wind should be perpendicular to the loops.

Each time the center reference point is crossed, the wings should be level, and the crossing angle should be the same.

Eights may be performed by rolling from one bank immediately to the other, directly over the center reference.

13.5 Eights Along a Road

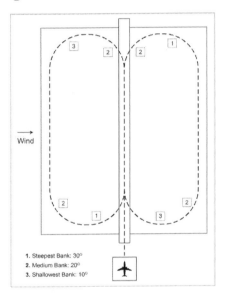

Find a road that is perpendicular to the wind. Aligning with the road will require you to determine a reference heading (wind-correction angle) to maintain the ground track along the road. Turning into the wind and subsequent turn with the wind will require you to vary the bank angle to maintain a constant-radius turn.

Roll rates should be consistent with how fast the groundspeed changes during the turn. Remember, when turning from an upwind or downwind position to a crosswind position, one-half of the groundspeed change occurs during the first two-thirds of the 90-degree turn. The

Ground Reference Maneuvers

final one-half of the change in groundspeed occurs during the last one-third of the turn.

In contrast, when turning from a crosswind position to an upwind or downwind position, the first one-half of the groundspeed change occurs during the first one-third of the 90-degree turn.

The final one-half of the change in groundspeed occurs during the last two-thirds of the turn. The straight-away portion will require another wind-correction angle to maintain your lateral separation from the road.

Ground Reference Maneuvers Brief

Ground Reference Maneuvers are required Pre-Solo Maneuvers. For all these maneuvers, the entry procedures are clearly stated in the ACS: the applicant must take into consideration the hazards of terrain, obstacles, appropriate airspace, other aircraft, and an emergency landing site if the need were to arise. Failure to address a possible landing site while performing this maneuver may result in the failure of this task.

Ground Reference Maneuvers should be addressed and performed to proficiency before the student's introduction to the traffic pattern at the solo stage. The traffic pattern is the most advanced Ground Reference Maneuver; and as such, it should logically be trained after the Ground Reference Maneuver lesson.

Pilots should spend most of their time looking outside the aircraft, only glancing inside to verify their bank and altitude/airspeed. The altimeter should not move. Any instrument that is moving is not telling you anything you need to know.

Immediately, while looking outside, make a pitch change for altitude, or a power change for airspeed. If the power setting is initially correct, you should not have to change it during the maneuver, and the airspeed should be stable. Your only variables should be bank, pitch, and roll rate during these maneuvers: bank for wind correction, pitch to keep the altimeter from moving, roll rate to maintain a constant radius turn.

LEARNING TO FLY - ESSENTIAL ELEMENTS

So, what Altitude should I expect to fly with Ground Reference Maneuvers?

These maneuvers should be performed low enough to the ground to be able to see the effects of the wind—between 600 to 1000 feet AGL.

Additionally, commercial pilot-requirements expect Ground Reference Maneuvers to be performed at **Pivotal Altitude**. It is not necessary for private pilots to know about Pivotal Altitude, but I will include the formula here so they will understand that Pivotal Altitude for Ground Reference Maneuvers applies nicely for them. It allows them to fly low to the ground at a safe altitude, complying with FAA regulations.

Pivotal Altitude = (MPH) Ground Speed squared divided by 15

Pivotal Altitude = (KTS) Ground Speed squared divided by 11.3

Chapter 14
Four Left Turning Tendencies

> Propeller-Driven Aircraft may experience Four Left Turning Tendencies upon takeoff that cause an unintended Left Turn or Yaw.

- P-Factor (Propeller)
- Spiraling Slipstream (Corkscrew Effect)
- Propeller Gyroscopic Precession
- Torque Reaction

Considered one of aviation's basic concepts, pilots need to be aware of and understand these Left Turning Tendencies to avoid a situation where the aircraft makes an unexpected change in attitude, as in yawing to the left upon takeoff and climbout phases.

The propeller creates thrust, which makes the aircraft fly, but it also can create these four, *unintended,* effects that cause the aircraft to pull to the left. Generally, you need "more right rudder" to pull the aircraft back onto the centerline during takeoff. Although easy to master, instructors must spend an adequate amount of time educating student pilots on how to combat these four tendencies.

LEARNING TO FLY - ESSENTIAL ELEMENTS

To gauge how much right rudder to use on your particular aircraft, practice rolling into some left and right turns. Foreknowledge of this information will make it easier to react when experiencing these Left Turning Tendencies.

14.1 P-Factor

P-Factor, also known as Asymmetric Loading, results from the descending blade experiencing a higher AOA than the ascending blade.

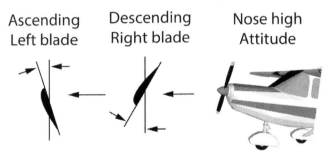

Asymmetric Propellar Loading (P-Factor)

In other words, the blade of the propeller that is descending will displace a larger amount of air when compared to the ascending blade.

When viewed from the cockpit, this results in a greater force being produced on the right (descending) blade compared to the left (ascending) blade. This causes subsequent Yaw to the left.

How to Counteract This Effect

This effect is noticeable only at high AOAs, such as those experienced during Slow Flight or Takeoff, and when taking off in a tailwheel aircraft. Regardless of when the P-Factor is experienced, right rudder input will be required as needed to maintain attitude.

Four Left Turning Tendencies

14.2 Spiraling Slipstream

The Slipstream created behind the propeller of an aircraft is displaced into a corkscrew pattern (Corkscrew Effect), meaning the Slipstream does not blow directly backward but "Spirals."

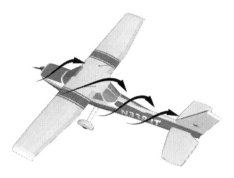

Spiraling Slipstream

This Spiraling Slipstream has the unintended consequence of striking (the technical term is "impinging") the vertical stabilizer (rudder) on the left side, which creates subsequent Yaw to the left. This effect is most noticeable during low-speed, high-power stages of flight, such as takeoff, where the propeller's Spiraling Slipstream is most significant compared to the total airflow over the vertical stabilizer. As total airflow over the vertical stabilizer increases compared to the propeller's Slipstream, this effect is reduced. In other words, if airspeed is **increased** and the Revolutions Per Minute (RPM) Setting is maintained, the Slipstream Effect will **decrease.**

How to Counteract This Effect

The Spiraling Slipstream effect can be counteracted by using right rudder input. For example, the Slipstream Effect (and subsequent Yaw) will increase when increasing power; therefore, simultaneous rudder input must be applied. When you increase power, slowly increase right rudder input, and vice versa.

14.3 Propeller Gyroscopic Precession

The properties of a Gyroscope apply to any spinning disc, and the aircraft's spinning propeller is no exception.

Gyroscopic Precession

A Gyroscope has two primary properties: rigidity in space and Precession. The exact mechanisms of how they function are beyond the scope of this brief, but a simplified summary of Precession is required to understand this tendency:

Precession causes a force applied to the propeller to be felt 90 degrees from the location of where the force is being applied, in the direction of rotation. In other words, if a propeller experiences a force in the 12 o'clock position, and the propeller is spinning in a clockwise direction, the force will be felt in the 3-o'clock position.

This force is significantly relevant only in the case of tailwheel aircraft during takeoff, where the rising of the aircraft's tail causes a force to be applied to the top of the propeller.

This force then **Precesses** and is felt on the right side of the propeller (when viewed from the cockpit), which causes a Yawing Tendency to the left. This effect also occurs when raising or lowering the aircraft's nose but is insignificant under normal circumstances.

Four Left Turning Tendencies

How to Counteract This Effect

During takeoff in a tailwheel aircraft, anticipate the Yaw to the left when the tail rises from the ground. When the tail rises, increase right rudder input. When in flight, apply rudder input as required if you notice the aircraft Yawing to the right when raising the nose or Yawing to the left when lowering the nose.

14.4 Torque Reaction

The Torque Effect is another byproduct of the clockwise rotation of the aircraft's propeller when viewed from the cockpit.

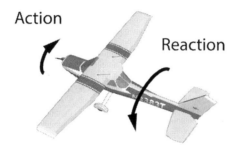

Torque Reaction

According to Newton's third law that states "for every action, there is an equal and opposite reaction," the clockwise rotation of the aircraft's propeller causes an opposite reaction in an anti-clockwise direction, which causes the aircraft to roll to the left during flight. On the ground, the Torque Effect causes increased friction on the left landing gear of an aircraft (due to the roll to the left), and this causes the aircraft to Yaw to the left.

How to Counteract This Effect

The Torque Effect is not particularly noticeable during flight unless power is increased quickly at a low airspeed and a high AOA. To counteract the left-roll effect, use right-aileron input as required.

Chapter 15
Special Takeoffs and Landings

> Eventually, you will fly into airports with short or soft runways, including dirt or grass. There is a special way to takeoff and land on these two types of runways.

A normal landing includes engine power, wind compensation, a firm surface on which to land, and ample runway space. A normal takeoff is defined in the same way, except for the unwanted possibility of engine failure. Likewise, performing successful Short Field and Soft Field Takeoffs and Landings are critical skills to master for every pilot seeking FAA certification.

All four of the following procedures need a high degree of proficiency in execution to safely complete each maneuver. Assume the runway surface is not a standard surface, with maybe some 50-foot trees at the departure or arrival end. Also taking into account the winds, gross weight of the aircraft, and density altitude calculation, these takeoff and landing procedures are aimed for such a situation.

CAVEAT: Pilots should always consult and follow the performance section of the AFM/POH to obtain the power settings, flap settings, airspeeds, and procedures prescribed by the aircraft's manufacturer.

LEARNING TO FLY - ESSENTIAL ELEMENTS

15.1 Short Field Takeoff with Obstacle

- Taxi to the Extreme End of Takeoff Area, Align Aircraft (nosewheel) with the Runway, Ensure Takeoff Flaps Set.

- Program the Wheel Slightly Aft and Apply Takeoff Power Smoothly and as Quickly as Practical.

- Apply Elevator Control to Keep the Weight Off the Nosewheel until Airspeed Accelerates to the Bottom of the Green Arc.

- Slowly Raise the Nose (three degrees per second) to the Best Angle of Climb Speed (**Vx speed attitude**) until Clear of Obstacle.

- Lower the Nose Attitude Slightly to Accelerate to the Best Rate of Climb (**Vy speed attitude**) and Slowly Retract the Flaps, Continue the Climb.

Short Field Takeoff with Obstacle

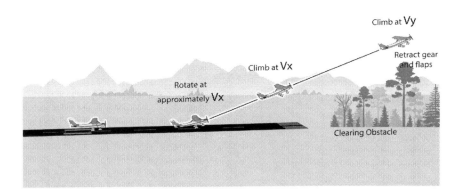

Special Takeoffs and Landings

Short Field Takeoff with Obstacle Brief

You must take off efficiently and make the steepest angle of climb that is safely possible after takeoff.

> As a rule of thumb, an aircraft's maximum Angle of Climb is at the speed of approximately 1.3 times the power-off stall speed, **but check the POH for the exact figure**.
>
> The maximum Angle of Climb gives you more altitude for the distance traveled forward, which is needed in this situation.

Begin at the extreme end of the runway, remembering the old aviation adage: "The runway behind you, the altitude above you, and the fuel you left back in the fuel truck are the three most useless items to a pilot."

Set the flaps as recommended by the manufacturer. Program the wheel or stick slightly aft and smoothly open the throttle. As you accelerate, program the elevator control to keep the weight off the nosewheel.

The objective is to lift off as soon as you can, but do not rush the process. Trying to hurry the aircraft off the ground will result in a high drag, slow takeoff, using up valuable runway distance. The aircraft will lift off when the minimum flying speed is attained.

If the field is rough, you want to lift off sooner than later, so keeping the weight off the nosewheel is desired. Nosewheel shimmy can also be a factor, especially in a rough field.

Once airborne, accelerate to best angle of climb speed (Vx) and climb beyond your 50-foot obstacle before assuming a normal climb attitude (Vy) with normal climb power, while slowly retracting the flaps.

LEARNING TO FLY - ESSENTIAL ELEMENTS

15.2 Short Field Landing with Obstacle

- Assume a Slightly Larger than Normal Traffic Pattern. Be on Final with Full Flaps at Final Approach Airspeed **(target airspeed)** and Appropriate **Descent Attitude**.

- Use Power to Control Glide, Your Airspeed, and Rate of Descent. When Clear of the Obstacle, Smoothly Reduce Power **Slightly** and Lower the Nose (descent attitude) to Maintain Target Airspeed. Do not raise the nose until you are ready to land.

- Touch Down on the Main Wheels, Power Off. Apply Heavy Braking and Retract Flaps to Put Most Weight on Main Landing Gear. (**Caution, when raising the flaps while in the landing phase of flight. I consider the use of this technique very much out of the norm. It should be used only if absolutely necessary.**) Careful Briefing of Landing Criteria and Execution is Required. Pilots Have Inadvertently Raised the Landing Gear Handle During this Procedure.

(Use slightly higher than normal approach Target Airspeed in turbulent air.)

Short Field Landing with Obstacle

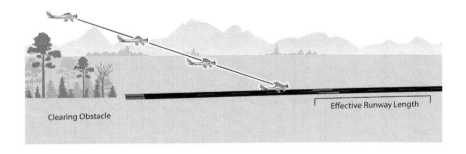

Clearing Obstacle · Effective Runway Length

Special Takeoffs and Landings

Short Field Landing with Obstacle Brief

The Short Field Approach is the most useful type of **Power Approach,** allowing the pilot to control the glide path to the aiming point and make a landing with a minimum of float.

"Ground Effect" becomes a factor when the aircraft is at about one-half wingspan distance from the ground, or about 18-20 feet for most aircraft. The downwash of the wing is changed with the result that induced drag is decreased by up to 48 percent in some cases. This is a considerable reduction of total drag just above the runway, which notably causes the aircraft to float.

When maneuvering properly, the aircraft will always land slightly past the aiming point or spot because of the rounding off of the landing. Aim for an approach speed that has a minimum amount of float, plus a definite margin of safety. Target airspeed should be flown on final (1.3 x Vso plus 5 kts, no wind).

The traffic pattern should be slightly wider and longer than normal at your DMMS speed until on final. Use power to control your airspeed and descent rate on final, gradually slowing to no lower than your Vref speed (1.3 x Vso) on final approach. Remember, your aiming point is not your touchdown point. Use power as needed to make the landing. It may be necessary to keep power on all the way to the ground if you get low and slow.

After landing, hold the control wheel (or stick) fully back as you apply braking. This helps put most of the weight on the main wheels and enhances aerodynamic braking efficiency. Knowing it could be a distraction, brief yourself as to the use of flap retraction on landing to kill some of the residual lift and put more weight on the wheels. Again, more than one pilot has inadvertently raised the landing gear handle during this time. Not a good thing.

Because of the effects of the wind, the aircraft's glide angle will differ as the winds vary. The glide angle in relation to the ground may change with each approach. By making a **Power Approach**, the pilot can then compensate for the wind while concentrating on the aiming point.

15.3 Soft Field Takeoff

- On Soft/Rough Field from Run-Up Area, Do Not Stop the Taxi.

- Leave the Run-Up Area with Full Nose-Up Elevator.

- Apply Takeoff Power when Aligned for Takeoff, Do Not Stop.

- Keep the Nose at **Vx Speed Attitude** on Main Wheels until Clear of the Ground.

- Once Airborne, Lower the Nose and Accelerate in Ground Effect until **Vx Airspeed,** then Climb until Clear of Obstacles. Lower Nose Slightly and Accelerate to Vy Best Rate of Climb Speed or Climb at Normal Climb Attitude, while Slowly Retracting Flaps.

Soft Field Takeoff Brief

With a contaminated runway (mud, snow, or tall grass), the drag on the wheels of the aircraft tends to make acceleration insufficient. The use of the Soft Field Takeoff Procedure here is a powerful tool.

The Soft Field Takeoff requires full aft wheel or stick while taxiing to the takeoff position, never stopping so as to prevent getting stuck on the takeoff surface. Use flaps recommended by the POH. Once in takeoff position, while still moving, apply full power keeping the wheel full aft to allow the aircraft to rise to the proper attitude, approximately the climb attitude. This will vary with different aircraft.

The objective is to become airborne as soon as possible without stalling. Once airborne, lower the nose below the climb attitude and allow the aircraft to accelerate in ground effect to a normal climb speed, or if obstacles, best angle of climb speed (Vx).

Special Takeoffs and Landings

Continue climbing until clear of all obstacles. Then accelerate to Vy best rate of climb speed or the normal climb attitude while slowly retracting the flaps.

15.4 Soft Field Landing

- Assume a Slightly Larger than Normal Pattern. Be on Final with Full Flaps and at Final Approach Airspeed **(target airspeed)** and **Descent Attitude**.

- Use Power to Control the Glide.

- Use Power to Touchdown with Minimum Sink Rate and Touch Down on Main Wheels.

- Use Power to Keep Rolling until Clear of Soft Area. Lower the Nose as Gently as Possible. Keep Full Aft Stick while Taxiing on the Soft Field.

Soft Field Landing Brief

A good landing always begins with a good approach; **do not make a short approach here.** Put yourself on a comfortable downwind position and slightly extend yourself to be on final with time to analyze your sight picture.

Avoid the mistake of being high and fast. A Soft Field Approach and Landing is not the time to rush.

The objective of the Soft Field Landing is to land as slowly as possible using power to control the descent rate. During this process, the nose needs to be in the climb position at touchdown with the wheel or stick being programmed full aft to keep the weight off the nosewheel.

Chapter 16
Airport Operations

> Knowing the Traffic Pattern helps pilots remain safe and organized, even if the airport has no ATC tower.

I mentioned earlier in the book that the Airport Traffic Pattern is an advanced Ground Maneuver. How can this be? Knowledge and proficiency in the Four Fundamentals of Flight, along with the fundamentals of attitude flying, are of paramount importance before you ever see a traffic pattern.

Pilots not schooled in the precise procedures of the Day-One Turn may execute Traffic Patterns resembling amoebas. Add to that tracking, correcting for the wind, air speed transitions during aircraft configuration changes, and the dreaded Go-Around Procedure now make the Traffic Pattern challenges significant.

One flight instructor, after being asked when to introduce Go-Arounds, confidently answered: during the takeoff and landing phases of training. In point of fact, the Go-Around Procedure should be introduced and briefed on Day-One of a student pilot's training. Maneuvers such

LEARNING TO FLY - ESSENTIAL ELEMENTS

as slow flight, stalls, and airspeed and slip descent demonstrations should be culminated with the Go-Around Procedure.

The Go-Around Procedure is the most important maneuver in a pilot's toolkit and must be completely mastered before a student takes their solo flight.

I require my students to practice at least four Go-Arounds on every flight, applying the Go-Around Procedure at the completion of every Stall, Slow Flight, Sideslip, and Forward Slip Descent. By the time a student finishes all pre-solo requirements and begins the traffic pattern phase of their training, they have already completed 20 to 30 Go-Arounds.

Any flight instructor that delays imparting knowledge and mastery of the Go-Around Procedure to their students—as well as other pre-solo requirements—until it's time to introduce the traffic pattern for "landing training" puts the student *way behind the curve*.

Reference the corresponding numbers on the adjacent diagram

1. Runway Heading Confirmation, Reference Heading (wind) determined, Lights on and clock (time) noted.

2. Airborne, Climb Attitude, Positive Rate Gear Up. Fly reference heading (runway track) or assigned heading. Flaps up as applicable. (Short and Soft field takeoffs: flaps up after clearing the obstacles).

After Takeoff Checklist called for at 400 feet (light aircraft and light jets), 800 to 1000 feet (transport jets), announce "After Takeoff Checklist" immediately after retracting the flaps, and later, once established on an altitude during a lull in activity, execute the checklist, calling it complete.

3. Three Hundred Feet Below Pattern Altitude (1000 feet light aircraft or 1500 feet jets) or pre-briefed local course rule non-standard altitude, perform the **Day-One Turn** if remaining in the pattern.

Airport Operations

16.1 The Anatomy of a Runway

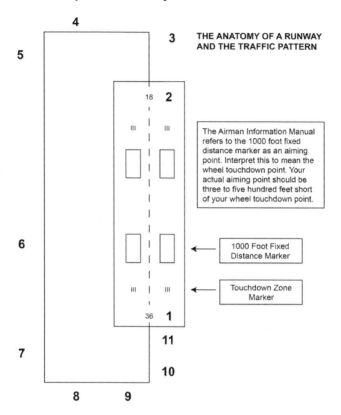

CAVEAT: If departing the pattern, no turns until the pattern altitude—either straight ahead or 45 degrees in the direction of the traffic pattern—are recommended at all airports. At towered fields you may be asked to perform traffic-pattern procedures at the direction or discretion of the ATC Controller. Standard Instrument Procedures, Engine Failure, and Obstacle-Clearance Procedures must be previously considered.

4. Perform the **Day-One Turn**.

5. Complete Level-Off Procedure. Maneuver aircraft the proper distance from the runway on downwind. Make the appropriate radio position report if applicable. Considering the wind, identify two points on the ground in line with the downwind track and compensate for the wind (Crab).

LEARNING TO FLY - ESSENTIAL ELEMENTS

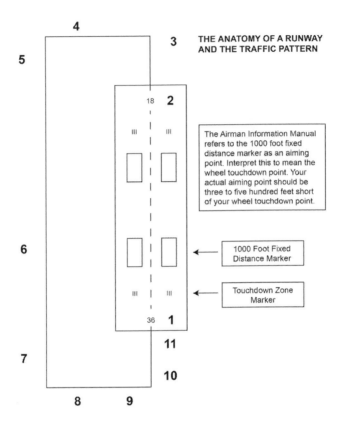

THE ANATOMY OF A RUNWAY AND THE TRAFFIC PATTERN

The Airman Information Manual refers to the 1000 foot fixed distance marker as an aiming point. Interpret this to mean the wheel touchdown point. Your actual aiming point should be three to five hundred feet short of your wheel touchdown point.

1000 Foot Fixed Distance Marker

Touchdown Zone Marker

6. Abeam the touchdown point, begin the aircraft landing configuration procedure. Once established at the DMMS for the flap setting, place the aircraft in the appropriate descent attitude and keep it there. Perform the landing checklist **(GUMPS)**.

7. Perform the **Day-One Turn**. In the turn, flaps as desired.

8. Ask yourself, "am I high or low?" Power and flaps as necessary.

9. Perform the **Day-One Turn**.

10. Aiming Point, Glideslope...Lineup...Airspeed, Descent Attitude. Repeat these words all the way to touchdown. Confirm that flaps and gear are down. Utilize Crab or Sideslip procedures to maintain the centerline at all times. There is never an excuse, regardless of the wind, for not having your body precisely on the extended centerline of the runway.

Airport Operations

Remember that an angling approach to the runway should *never* be an acceptable norm for any pilot.

Once in the flare, your **Sideslip Procedure** is *paramount* to maintain the centerline. Landing in a Crab will only exacerbate the undesirable side load on the landing gear. Remember, the aiming point is not your touchdown point. Utilize your pre-briefed aiming point so you can successfully land on your touchdown point.

11. Confirm appropriate stabilized sink rate (rate of descent). Don't raise the nose above the descent attitude until ready to land. Raise the nose to fly formation above the runway, ensuring your power is at idle. If the aircraft begins to sink, subtle adjustments in attitude from the level attitude to the climb attitude are necessary to keep the aircraft from touching down, the objective being able to land as slowly as possible.

Do Not Climb. If you begin to climb, quickly readjust the attitude with slight forward-elevator pressure to stop the climb, then immediately adjust to the climb attitude. Do not raise the nose above the climb attitude (the top of the glareshield on the horizon). Slip left or right with the ailerons to maintain the centerline using the rudder to keep the nose pointed straight down the runway.

Do not stop flying the aircraft once on the ground. Program the yoke or stick full aft to utilize aerodynamic braking. Wind correction and centerline track while slowing must be maintained. Execute judicial application of the brakes. There is never a reason to slam on the brakes during touchdown.

If you always have an aiming point and a touchdown point, you should never have to use the brakes, in most scenarios, until you have slowed significantly. I've often witnessed experienced pilots slamming on the brakes at touchdown either in the simulator or on the line. I attribute this to a poor habit-pattern without thought. **Remember,** one flies with the brain. Fly the aircraft all the way to the chocks!

Never begin or continue an approach without thinking about the Go-Around Procedure.

Guard against "Planned Continuation Bias," the unconscious cognitive bias to continue with the original plan in spite of changing conditions.

16.2 The Three Airport Approach Gates

Upon arrival to your destination airport, all aircraft must pass through two of three gates (windows) before landing. That is, First Gate, then Third Gate, or Second Gate, then Third Gate.

All aircraft must pass through the third gate (50 feet over the runway threshold) to complete the landing.

The **First and Second Gates** require the aircraft to be placed in the landing configuration at or before reaching either of those gates, respectively. Whether you prepare well before reaching the respective gate, or you commence the configuration change at the gate; remember, a stabilized approach is the goal when making preparation for the final descent.

You should be stabilized on your target airspeed (Vref + five kts or Vref + wind additive) and glideslope by 500 feet AGL if in VMC conditions, or 1000 feet AGL if in IMC conditions. It is imperative that you know how to recognize each gate and the procedures required at each of these points.

First Gate: Abeam the Touchdown Point. Fly approximately 30 seconds past the first gate before turning base. Once completing the base turn ask yourself, "am I high or low?" by visualizing an imaginary glideslope, referencing your aiming point. Make corrections as necessary to stay on the glideslope. The sooner, the better.

Second Gate: Straight In or Modified Base Approach. This requires the pilot to visualize an imaginary glideslope from an aiming point on the runway, or reference an electronic glideslope, and begin the final descent at the intersection of that glideslope.

Airport Operations

Third Gate: 50 feet above the Runway Threshold.

Be advised, the **First or Second Gate** is the geographical point where you begin your descent on the final approach. The aircraft should commence or be completely configured in the landing condition by this point. The aircraft must be stabilized by 500 feet above the runway surface on the approach path (glideslope).

Landing Gear Considerations

When, where, and why to put the landing gear in the down position directly relates to what I have emphasized throughout this treatise: executing a procedure or task until it becomes an automatic and integral part of a pilot's way of thinking and response is crucial to the pilot's development.

My technique has always been to mentally correlate the position of the landing gear with the arrival of the First Gate (abeam) or Second Gate (descent on the final approach). This thinking allows you to close a mental loop that the landing gear is in the down and locked position.

If you choose to configure the landing gear earlier, I would strongly suggest making one last check at the first or second gate, i.e., mentally tie your Landing Gear Handle with each of these gates.

What is worse than a gear-up landing? Some would say a second gear-up landing. There are pilots walking around with one gear-up landing, and there are some pilots with more than one. You definitely do not want to be that person.

Chapter 17
Emergency Operations

> Every aircraft's information manual has a section marked "Emergency Procedures" which should be regularly reviewed and understood along with "Critical Action Items" committed to memory.

Pilots should always be reviewing, assessing, and continuously learning their craft. Many magazines and publications tailored to aviation subjects are available. There are also online videos and FAA-website resources structured around the FAA Wings Pilot Proficiency Program to provide pilots the opportunity to remain current.

Note that very little in aviation is more important than a complete understanding of current Emergency Practices and Procedures. An "Emergency Procedures Review" should be a regularly scheduled part of a pilot's repertoire.

The key to successful management of an emergency situation from progressing into a true emergency is a thorough familiarity with, and adherence to, the procedures developed by the aircraft manufacturer. **The following guidelines are generic and are not meant to replace the approved AFM/POH procedures.**

LEARNING TO FLY - ESSENTIAL ELEMENTS

17.1 Engine Failure - The Four S's

1. Speed

- Aircraft Pitch Attitude to Best Glide Speed. (TRIM)
- **MAYDAY, MAYDAY, MAYDAY! (Emergency)**

2. Spot

- Pick a Spot to Land and Turn Toward It. (don't be afraid to turn the plane while looking for a place to land) If **IFR**, or on ATC Flight Following, ask ATC for the nearest airport

3. Start

- Switch Fuel Tanks
- Mixture - Rich
- Fuel Pump - On
- Carb Heat - On
- Magneto – Change

4. Shutdown

- Fuel Off
- Mixture - Off
- Master Switch – Off (only if you are finished communicating)
- Magnetos - Off
- Door - Crack Open

Radioing **"MAYDAY, MAYDAY, MAYDAY"** signals the situation has deteriorated to the point of "grave and imminent" danger.

Radioing **"PAN, PAN, PAN" (Possible Assistance Needed)** informs ATC, including emergency services as well as other aircraft, that an urgent problem exists.

Emergency Operations

17.2 Confirmed Fire in the Air / Emergency Descent

- Carburetor Heat **ON**, Power **Idle**
- Roll into a 45-degree Bank, Begin Descent
- Maintain Airspeed at Top of the White Arc
- Communicate with ATC: Squawk 7700 **MAYDAY, MAYDAY, MAYDAY (Emergency)**
- If Possible, Isolate and Control the Fire by securing electrical devices if an electrical fire, or securing the fuel if an engine fire
- Land as Soon as Possible (within 15 minutes)

17.3 Four Events Requiring Expedited Action

One should never be in a hurry if an abnormal condition presents itself in an aircraft. There are only **Four Times** you absolutely need to be in a hurry in an aircraft:

1. Confirmed Fire on the Ground or in the Air

Ground: If you suspect a fire, continue cranking to draw the fire into the engine. Keep the engine running for a few minutes, then shut down and inspect for damage. If the fire is out of control, immediately shut down the engine and evacuate the aircraft.

Airborne: (sec. 17.2)

2. High Speed Aborted Takeoff

The general procedure for an aborted (rejected) takeoff is simple: Power Idle, Maintain Directional Control, Maximum (if necessary) Braking. Keep in mind, however, that you should always follow the procedure your aircraft manufacturer recommends.

Announce **"ABORT, ABORT, ABORT,"** while bringing the power to idle. Depending on the runway length available, winds, weather, and weight of the aircraft, you should have already briefed and known how much

LEARNING TO FLY - ESSENTIAL ELEMENTS

braking you would need under the circumstances. Avoid slamming on the brakes if it is not necessary.

3. Low to the Ground with a Complete Power Loss

Immediately position the nose to the Descent Attitude to conserve airspeed for the flare. If time is available, immediately switch fuel tanks, confirm mixture rich and boost pump on. Depending on where this power loss occurred, you should have briefed and known what your best options would be, considering the weather, winds, runway condition, aircraft weight, and terrain.

Important: After just taking off, unless you are above a specified altitude from your previous brief, you should never try to perform the ***Impossible Turn** back to the airport. If the Impossible Turn is viable (you are high enough), make sure you turn into the wind to keep yourself inside the airport boundary.

Everything else is irrelevant if your nose is not in the Descent Attitude. You will need to feel a lightness in your seat as you program the yoke for a Nose-Down Descent Attitude. You will probably be below Best Glide Speed. Getting the descent attitude quickly will preserve what little speed you will need for a final flare.

Unless you establish that glide, there is no time for anything else. Case studies by the FAA show that four seconds is the average reaction time in an emergency. Less experienced pilots will take longer to recognize an emergency situation.

---

* **The Impossible Turn:** a risky maneuver attempted when an aircraft's engine fails during climbout. It involves a steep bank at low airspeed and a turn of more than 180 degrees to return to the runway. If the emergency occurs at a low altitude, you likely won't have enough energy to successfully execute it. It is essential to prioritize safety and follow recommended procedures after an engine failure during takeoff.

Emergency Operations

Finally, if you wait until an engine failure occurs to think about it, it is probably too late. If the engine burps for any reason, you should be spring-loaded to the Descent Attitude.

4. Low to the Ground Upside Down

If you find yourself in this situation, e.g., wind shear event, wake turbulence, flight control abnormal, etc., your outcome will primarily be based on your energy (airspeed and altitude) and your reaction time. At the very least, you need to unload the wing with forward stick (yoke) pressure while aggressively rolling the aircraft with full rudder and aileron.

There is no time to consider aircraft configuration. Once upright, continue unloading the wing in the Descent Attitude with full power until you are able to regain aircraft control.

Once in control, the Go-Around Procedure would be very necessary and appropriate.

17.4 Declaring Minimum Fuel and Emergency Fuel

In preparation for a flight, FAR 91.103 addresses a pilot's responsibility to know all pertinent information about the upcoming flight that includes weather, fuel requirements, known traffic delays and so forth.

Armed with this information and safety always being paramount, the pilot can now confidently begin the flight understanding that its outcome should never be in doubt.

> Solid ADM along with a host of other Single Pilot Resource Management (SRM) tools and procedures were designed to mitigate or eliminate any threats.

Aviation mishaps occur due to fuel starvation or fuel exhaustion. The FAA has provided a method pilots can think about and utilize when any scenario concerning fuel may be an issue. **"Minimum Fuel"** and **"Emergency Fuel"** are two terms a pilot must thoroughly understand in both knowledge and execution. It matters not whether a flight is VFR or IFR, unfortunate or disastrous consequences have occurred only because the pilot did not communicate a fuel concern with ATC.

It is concerning that in all levels of aviation there seems to be a disconnect among pilots about the meaning and application of these two terms. I have personally discussed this with high-time, professional pilots who were unaware of the terms, much less how to appropriately apply them.

My experience flying westbound across the ocean in the wintertime and against the jet stream often necessitated the "Minimum Fuel" declaration hours before reaching our final destination. It matters not where or how far your flight leg is in time; what matters is recognizing that you may have a fuel situation. Unforecasted headwinds, unexpected traffic delays, reroutes, suspected fuel leaks, confirmed fuel leaks, engine-out incidents, and other scenarios have occurred and will continue to occur.

FAR 91.151 addresses VFR fuel requirements, and FAR 91.167 addresses IFR requirements. These regulations apply to preflight and dispatch procedures.

Once airborne, solid ADM practices should provide the path to maintain these requirements. However, experiencing a fuel scenario placing 91.151 or 91.167 in jeopardy is a concern.

For Example: I once asked my First Officer to declare Minimum Fuel to ATC. ATC then requested our fuel state to which the First Officer erroneously replied with an inflated number. Upon querying him as to why the incorrect fuel reading, he stated that he was complying with the 45-minute reserve requirement. *Of course, we had an enlightening talk at the end of the flight.* When ATC asks you for your fuel state, it is not a wish list.

Emergency Operations

The Aeronautical Information Manual (AIM) defines "Minimum Fuel Status" as when your fuel supply has reached a state where you cannot accept any undue delay in reaching your destination.

Continuing, it states that this is not an emergency situation, but merely an advisory that indicates an emergency situation is possible should any undue delay occur. The key here is knowing that a declaration of Minimum Fuel does not imply a need for "Traffic Priority."

If the "Minimum Fuel Advisory" negates ATC traffic handling priorities, why bother declaring it? This is where the misconception happens. Remember when my First Officer gave ATC our inaccurate fuel state believing he needed to be in compliance with FAR 91.167? He failed to understand that it is perfectly legal to land with low fuel as long as ATC has previously been notified of a minimum fuel state; and if needed, an "Emergency Fuel Declaration" at the appropriate time.

Declaring the "Minimum Fuel Advisory," in nature only, is there to protect you, the pilot, if any situation occurs. What you cannot do is complete an entire flight, knowing that fuel may be a concern, and finally declare "Emergency Fuel" to ATC.

Springing an "Emergency Fuel Declaration" at the last minute without giving ATC a "Heads Up Minimum Fuel Declaration," in most cases, may find you vulnerable for a "*709" ride by the FAA.

Practicing responsible CRM/SRM (ch. 18), means not keeping others in the dark. The Minimum Fuel and Emergency Fuel declarations need to be thoroughly taught and understood.

Remember, waiting for an engine to quit, while knowing you are already low on fuel is an *inappropriate time* to declare a fuel problem without having previously declared "Minimum Fuel." There continues to be an absurd abundance of "too little, too late," incidents like this

---

* A 709 Ride is a **Jeopardy Ride** conducted by the FAA to reevaluate a pilot's certifications and rating. It is authorized under USC 44709 and can occur due to pilot actions or other reasons.

happening in our skies. This subject needs to be clearly emphasized in our basic aviation training.

Chapter 18
SRM: Single Pilot/Crew Resource Management

> SRM/CRM is the effective use of all available resources by the pilot or flight crew personnel to reduce error, avoid stress, and assure a safe and efficient operation.

Single Pilot Resource Management (SRM) is an adaptation of Crew Resource Management (CRM) training designed to apply to Single-Pilot Operations. SRM is the art of managing all onboard and outside resources available to the pilot before and during a flight to help ensure a successful outcome. By teaching pilots about their own human limitations, SRM aims to reduce the number of aviation accidents caused by human error.

ADM is considered a subsidiary concept of SRM. It is all about making good decisions based on valid inputs derived from SRM resources: communication skills, flight manuals, computers, other crew members, ATC, maintenance, line personnel, and a host of other resources collected from preflight to tie-down.

Good ADM depends on good SRM which includes concepts of Risk Management, Controlled Flight into Terrain (CFIT) Awareness, and SA. For example, most CFIT accidents occur in the approach and landing phase of the flight and may involve heavy pilot workload, weather, turbulence, icing, or a loss of SA.

A disciplined approach to SRM and ADM mitigates threats and ensures a safe and successful flight.

* * *

18.1 Pilot/Crew/Passenger Resource Management

Pilot-Crew Briefs

Taxi Plan

Runway Condition: Wet/Dry/Contaminated?

Abort Take-Off Criteria: Engine Failure, Safety of Flight Issues

Abort Procedure: Announce "ABORT, ABORT, ABORT." Power to Idle. Gradually Apply the Brakes as Needed

In Case of Engine Failure Below 1000 Feet:
Stick Forward (descent attitude)
Land Ahead Full Flaps (slow as practical)
In Case of Partial Power Engine Failure (not developing full power), Discuss the Impossible Turn

Normal Departure: Noise Abatement if Applicable (always comply with specific airport departure procedures)

Three-Step Change of Control:
Non-Pilot Flying: "I have the Controls."
Pilot Flying: "You have the Controls."
Non-Pilot Flying: "I have the Controls."

SRM: Single Pilot/Crew Resource Management

Passenger Brief

S – Seat Belts, Shoulder Harness, Seat Position
A – Air-Vents, Environmental Controls
F – Fire Extinguisher
E – Exit Doors, Emergency Evac Plan, Emergency Survival Kit
T – Traffic, Sterile Cockpit
Y – Your Questions

Single Pilot/Crew Resource Management Brief

SRM/CRM is a valuable tool for all aviation professionals and amateurs alike because its use and application accomplish many things, such as preflight preparation, flight management, the trapping of errors, communication, and checklist usage to name a few. And there are many more. An understanding of how to perceive the concept and utilize the tools provided with SRM/CRM can enhance and promote a safer operation.

Perception begins with how we receive and communicate information. **It's important to understand that you are not alone even if you are flying in the middle of the night and you are the only person onboard.** Realize that many people and resources are available from days before the flight through preflight, takeoff, cruise, approach, and landing. How we collect this information and utilize its particulars will determine how efficient we are as pilots and crewmembers.

Knowing we all perceive data in different ways, let us establish a common ground to accurately process this data and give us a desired pathway forward. What is required?

Given a scenario, how does one normally respond? A class of 30 people were given a test of 100 questions delineating different behavioral situations (see diagram on the next page). An example would be: you are walking down the street and a person sitting on the sidewalk sticks his foot out and trips you. How would you respond? Three answers were provided:

LEARNING TO FLY - ESSENTIAL ELEMENTS

- Answer number one was **aggressive** in nature, eg., a dirty look or something said by the walker in an aggressive manner.
- Answer number two was **nurturing** in nature, eg., "I'm okay; are you okay?"
- Answer number three was **autonomous** in nature, meaning a total unawareness of the person on the sidewalk. The walker just keeps going straight ahead, totally oblivious to what just happened.

CRM SAMPLE GRAPH

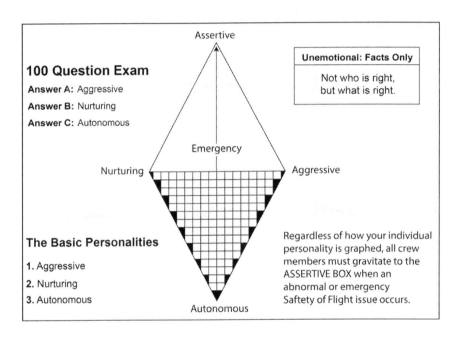

All 100 questions followed the same format. When the exams were processed and the answers were graphed on a matrix, it showed the class exhibiting trends from all three behavioral categories.

The PhD behaviorist was basically demonstrating that every person has his/her own personality. By choosing one of three ways to handle a situation, you are demonstrating one of three personalities: **aggressive,**

SRM: Single Pilot/Crew Resource Management

nurturing, or **autonomous**. Simply put, everyone has a basic personality, some more aggressive than others.

Is it okay to exercise these differing traits in today's flight deck? Here is the significance: one cannot change his/her personality; it is what it is. But when the rubber meets the road with an emergency coming up in flight, what do we really need in the aircraft?

1. You **do not** need an **aggressive** individual who may make a wrong decision in haste without considering the input of others.
2. You **do not** need a **nurturing** individual who may make the decision as to what needs to be done in an untimely fashion.
3. You **do not** need an **autonomous** individual in a world of his/her own with no idea of what is happening.

Be Assertive!

The PhD behaviorist demonstrated that every personality type needs to gravitate to the "assertive" box.

The characteristics of the assertive box are:

- First, no emotion
- Second, it is not who is right, but what is right

The PIC must be able to receive and share all available data, and the crewmembers must be able to equally receive and share all pertinent data. During an emergency or a highly-stressful situation, the people involved need to understand the importance of accessing the feedback coming in and of making the correct response in an assertive manner.

In a Single-Pilot Environment, the PIC needs to act according to this Assertive Manner with all the people at his/her disposal, whether it be the tower, approach, departure, center control, crew, or a passenger. Personality type of an individual *should not* have a prominent role in how that person exercises his/her situation in an assertive way.

Sometimes things may get heated with controllers and crewmembers; however, knowing the aforementioned behavioral categories, and how those behaviors may influence a situation, should provide a clear understanding of how to navigate high-stress events using an **Assertive Approach** without adverse emotional behavior, which leads to good communication, accurate perceptions, and positive outcomes.

In conclusion, you are not going to change someone's personality. What the PhDs are saying is that it's okay to have differing personalities. When things are going smoothly, differing personalities should not have much of an effect on a flight.

What the airlines, the military, and the corporate and charter world desire is that when the situation in the aircraft becomes tenuous or threatening, pilots and crews need to gravitate to the **Assertive Box**. It is not who is right, but what is right. All pilots and crewmembers should be exposed to this powerful philosophy.

18.2 Risk Management Models and Checklists

The following sampling of models and checklists provided by the FAA is derived from the **Four Fundamentals Risk Elements: Pilot, Aircraft, Environment, and Type of Operation** to assist pilots and crews in mitigating threats associated with flight operations.

3P Model for Aeronautical Decision Making (ADM)

- **Perceive:** recognize if a conflict exists between supporting instruments that suggests a potential failure.
- **Process:** determine how significant an effect this potential failure would have on flight safety.
- **Perform:** verify the failure and implement the best possible course of action to continue the flight safely, or terminate the flight early in the interest of safety.

Reminder: ME: Mitigate or Eliminate, Evaluate

SRM: Single Pilot/Crew Resource Management

Pave Checklist: A Primary Tool for Risk Management in Flight Planning

- **P**ilot: evaluate your competency to safely conduct the flight, e.g., health, stress, fatigue, emotional state.
- **A**ircraft: consider the limitations of the aircraft, e.g., inoperative components, aircraft airworthiness.
- en**V**ironment: more than just weather, e.g., terrain, available ATC services, ground services, etc.
- **E**xternal Pressures: faulty decision-making that can compromise the safety of the flight.

For each element, list the risks, or combination of risks, that can be managed safely and successfully.

Decide Model for Aeronautical Decision Making: A Logical Progression

- **D**etect: recognizes the PIC has detected a change has occurred.
- **E**stimate: acknowledges the PIC's urgency to react to the change.
- **C**hoose: suggests the PIC should select a desirable outcome for the flight.
- **I**dentify: the PIC identifies the steps necessary to successfully deal with the change.
- **D**o: the PIC performs the steps necessary for the situation.
- **E**valuate: the PIC evaluates the result of his/her actions.

The **Decide Model Scenario** should be performed more than just once; it is a looping process of thoughts and actions that repeats, starting with **"Detect"** each time a change is recognized.

You, as the PIC, are the last line of defense. It is critically important that you carefully consider these elements before you fly.

LEARNING TO FLY - ESSENTIAL ELEMENTS

Five Hazardous Attitudes

- **Anti-authority (autonomous):** A self-imposed isolation
- **Impulsivity (rushing):** Lack of consideration before taking action
- **Invulnerability (invincible):** It won't happen to me
- **Macho (I can do it):** A dangerous thought process
- **Resignation (what's the use?):** Causes inaction

Experts have identified these "Hazardous Attitudes" as the most common roadblocks to safe and successful flying outcomes.

5P Model to Systematically Assess Pertinent Risks to Flight

- **P**lan: gather all pertinent information as it relates to the route, fuel requirements, weather, NOTAMs, etc.
- **P**lane: verify aircraft's mechanical fitness; be familiar with its systems/operations; organize paperwork.
- **P**ilot: realistically self-evaluate your health, fatigue, stress levels, and any medications taken.
- **P**assengers: know your passengers and recognize how to deal with them in various flight situations.
- **P**rogramming: verify the integrity and currency of databases and software you are using.

I'm Safe Checklist to Evaluate Your Fitness for a Flight

    I – Illness
    M – Medication
    S – Stress
    A – Alcohol
    F – Fatigue
    E – Emotion

Chapter 19
Communications

> Effective communication plays a crucial role in ensuring the seamless flow of information between pilots, crewmembers, ATC, and ground personnel. Radio discipline and a high knowledge of radio terminology are essential for effective communication.

Flying is a lot about confidence. Garnering as much knowledge and skill in all facets of aviation—especially radio communication—will provide a level of confidence and flying enjoyment for the rest of your aviation career. It is essential for every pilot to become familiar with the terminology of this chapter.

Pilots should strive to improve their Radio Transmissions, remembering that the less said, the better. Be concise and do not "garbage up" the radio frequency. Take the opportunity to listen to real-time ATC radio transmissions like LiveATC.net.

Included in this chapter is a very specific order of operation when transmitting a radio call. Carefully craft each transmission based upon the order of the transmission. This is a powerful tool with which to enhance your communication skills.

LEARNING TO FLY - ESSENTIAL ELEMENTS

19.1 Communicating with ATC and other Aircraft

First, Pilots Must Know the "Phonetic Alphabet"

Letter	Code Word	Letter	Code Word
A	Alfa	N	November
B	Bravo	O	Oscar
C	Charlie	P	Papa
D	Delta	Q	Quebec
E	Echo	R	Romeo
F	Foxtrot	S	Sierra
G	Golf	T	Tango
H	Hotel	U	Uniform
I	India	V	Victor
J	Juliet	W	Whiskey
K	Kilo	X	X-ray
L	Lima	Y	Yankee
M	Mike	Z	Zulu

The creation of the **"Phonetic Alphabet"** can be traced back to WWI when wired telephones were used on the battlefield. Static and noisy conditions necessitated the creation of this code to distinguish Bs from Vs, As from 8s, etc. Since aeronautical radio transmissions are also inhibited by crackly radios, it makes sense to use this great resource.

The International Civil Aviation Organization (ICAO) developed the current phonetic alphabet system in the 1950s, and the FAA quickly adopted it. **Pilots must practice this code until it is "second nature," meaning to be able to use it without thinking.**

The quickest way to commit the phonetic alphabet to memory is with the use of flash cards. You will be surprised at how much you retain just from the initial creation of these cards. Flash cards are an extremely effi-

Communications

cient training tool that enhances and encourages active recall. Get in the habit of running through the cards each night before bedtime, along with any other practices and procedures you are trying to commit to memory.

The Second Item to Consider when Communicating with ATC or other Aircraft is When to Use Your Full Call Sign (Tail Number).

If you initiate the transmission while airborne, use your full call sign. If someone else initiates the transmission to you, repeat their response or request **followed** by your full call sign.

Abbreviate your call sign only when ATC first initiates the abbreviation. When on the ground, always use your full call sign.

The **Order** of the transmission is to use your full call sign with the first transmission followed by the identification of the controller or pilot you are trying to call.

Once someone has responded to your transmission, read back the appropriate response first, followed by your call sign. That way you will not be as prone to forget what was read to you. Sometimes clearances or instructions can be quite lengthy, so you need to stick the call sign at the end of the transmission.

If the controller calls you first, simply read back what is appropriate and stick your call sign at the end of the transmission.

Remember, if someone calls you, make it easy on yourself; stick your call sign at the end of your response. Say your call sign first only if you are initiating the first radio transmission.

My favorite Pilot to Controller responses:

Say Again: Self Explanatory.

Confirm: (ex. when questioning a controller): "Tower, **confirm** that previous transmission was for 83 Tango."

Roger: To acknowledge only. Does not mean yes or no!

<u>Concur</u>: Agree (ex. when the controller identifies your position): You would answer **concur,** and then state your call sign.

<u>Assigned</u>: (ex. when previously assigned by the last controller): On a new approach frequency, you would check in including your heading and the word "assigned."

At Non-Towered Airports (airborne or on the ground) your transmission should include the following:

Who they are
Who you are
Where you are
State your "Intentions"
Who they are

Pop-Up Report: checking in with a controlling-agency's radar:
Who they are
Who you are
"Request"

Pop-Up Report: after ATC responds:
Who they are
Who you are
Type aircraft
Position
Altitude
State your "Intentions or Requests"

19.2 Forty Must Know Pilot/ATC Radio Phrases for VFR Pilots

The following is a handpicked list of pilot and ATC phrases and examples for VFR pilots (student, private, etc.) who don't have a lot of experience with radio communications.

Communications

Many terms and phrases used on the radio don't have obvious meanings. This guide is meant to help with that; although, this list is not exhaustive. The complete Pilot/Controller Glossary may be found online at www.faa.gov/air_traffic/publications/media/pcg_4-03-14.pdf.

It is imperative to study these terms and commit them to memory.

Basic Radio Communications

A Tip for Student Pilots: Always identify yourself to controllers as a Student Pilot. Controllers want to help you and will be better able to accommodate you if they know you are a student pilot.

Acknowledge

If asked to acknowledge by controllers, it means they want you to confirm that you understood their latest instruction. The best way to acknowledge is to say "roger" and simply repeat the instructions you were given. If you didn't understand the instructions, you can ask them to repeat the instructions by using the phrase "say again."

Affirmative

Affirmative simply means…yes. Was this term easy to learn? Affirmative.

Blocked or Stepped On

Used to describe when a radio transmission was not readable due to multiple radio transmissions on the same frequency. This is also known as "stepping on" others. If two people transmit at the same time, they are both stepping on each other.

Expedite

Quite simply…hurry up. If you are told to expedite some instruction from ATC, it means to comply promptly and do what they say for the sake of safety. Always remember, however, that you should never compromise your or your passenger's safety. If you can't perform what is being asked by ATC, tell them you are "unable."

LEARNING TO FLY - ESSENTIAL ELEMENTS

How Do You Hear Me?

This is a question that can be asked by a pilot or controller to another pilot or controller about the quality of their radio transmission. A good transmission can be answered with "loud and clear," but a bad transmission can be met with "garbled" or "barely readable."

Monitor

Many times, ATC will tell pilots to monitor frequencies. One of the most common examples is that after landing, a pilot will be told "taxi to the ramp and monitor ground point six." Monitor means to switch to the frequency and listen to await further instructions. In the case of "ground point six" we would switch our radios to 121.6 (121 is the "ground" frequency) and listen as we taxi to the ramp.

Negative

The official way to say...no. Opposite of affirmative.

No Joy-Looking

Used to inform the Air Traffic Controller you are unable to see reported traffic in your vicinity.

Roger

"Roger" means I have received and understand your radio transmission. It is not a yes or no, like affirmative or negative. It's simply an acknowledgement of hearing and understanding. Don't use "roger" in place of "affirmative."

Say Again

A request to repeat the previous radio transmission, most likely due to a misunderstanding in communications.

Unable

Simply, the pilot cannot comply with a request from ATC, or ATC cannot grant a request from a pilot.

Communications

<u>Wilco</u>

Short for "will comply." It means you have heard the request and will comply with the instructions given to you. Example: ATC requests "report passing 8000." Your response: "Wilco, 8000." (Respond to any report command with Wilco.)

Airport Operations

<u>Back Taxi</u>

This is an instruction given by ATC, or pilots can request if needed, to taxi on the runway the opposite direction of the flow of take-offs/landings. It may be used to increase available runway distance for takeoff, and there may be times where you should request it if you need it. It is also an instruction given to us by ATC after landing. Oftentimes, you'll be instructed to "make a 180 and back taxi" to exit a runway.

<u>Braking Action</u>

Braking action is the effectiveness of the brakes on the runway and airport surfaces when it is snowing or raining heavily. If precipitation has caused the runways and taxiways to be slick, braking action will be given a rating such as poor or nil. If it is okay, it will be given a good report. Braking action reports will often be mentioned in the Automatic Terminal Information Service (ATIS) broadcasts and should be noted when approaching an airport. The ICAO has adopted a standardized system for reporting runway conditions to pilots. Refer to the Runway Conditions Assessment Matrix (RCAM).

<u>Cleared for the Option</u>

The "option" gives the pilot discretion to do whatever he/she desires during an approach and landing. This includes the option to touch and go, low approach, missed approach, stop and go, or a full stop landing. This clearance is often given to pilots by ATC when they are at a controlled airport and have the traffic pattern to themselves with no other aircraft in the vicinity.

LEARNING TO FLY - ESSENTIAL ELEMENTS

Closed Traffic

Assigned by the tower, it means successive trips around the traffic pattern in which the pilot does not exit the pattern.

Go-Around

A procedure in which a pilot abandons an approach to land, and reconfigures the aircraft to climb. This usually includes adding power, and slowly "cleaning up" the aircraft configuration.

Sometimes ATC will order pilots to go around if there is a safety concern. Many times, this will be another aircraft on the runway, but it could also be for a variety of other reasons.

You may also decide to initiate a Go-Around if you determine that you cannot safely land. In situations of extreme crosswinds for example, it may be wise to abort a landing, go around, and try again.

Know that the Go-Around Procedure is more about placing the aircraft in a known, safe, flying state as discussed in chapter six.

Land and Hold Short Operation (LAHSO)

When listening to ATIS, you will often hear "land and hold short operations are in effect." LAHSO are used at airports with intersecting runways or taxiways, and aircraft are instructed to land and hold short of a specific location on the field. Usually the "hold short point" is a runway, but can also be a taxiway, or the approach/departure end of another runway.

As PIC, you have authority to accept or reject the LAHSO instruction.

Be advised, student pilots on solo flights are not authorized to accept LAHSO instructions.

Before accepting a LAHSO clearance, make sure you can safely meet the demand placed on you and your aircraft. Keep in mind landing distance requirements for your aircraft, and your ability to land at the necessary spot on the runway.

Communications

<u>Line Up and Wait</u>

"Line up and wait" is the instruction given to a pilot just before take-off. It means to literally taxi onto the runway, line up with the runway centerline, and wait for further instruction. Obviously, the next instruction given is "cleared for takeoff" unless unforeseen circumstances come into play to prevent a takeoff.

Many times, this instruction will be issued when it is necessary to wait on other aircraft to taxi clear of the active runway, cross the active runway, there is traffic at the departure end of the runway, or wake turbulence is a factor from a heavy aircraft taking off or landing.

<u>Low Approach</u>

A low approach is an approach to landing where a go-around is initiated before landing and the aircraft does not touch the ground.

<u>Make Short Approach</u>

Sometimes you will be asked to "make short approach" while practicing landings in closed traffic. This is an abbreviated downwind, base, and final leg of a traffic pattern used to get on the ground quicker than the standard traffic pattern. Sometimes it is requested from ATC to pilots for traffic separation, and other times we pilots will request short approaches if we are practicing power-off 180s to simulate engine failures.

<u>Progressive Taxi</u>

Requesting progressive taxi instructions from ATC is another way of asking for precise, step-by-step instructions on how to reach a location on the ground. It can be used if you are at an unfamiliar airport and want to prevent getting lost on the ground.

Do your homework and study the airport diagrams before arriving at an airport so you don't absolutely need to request progressive taxi. Think of it as a backup service that you can request if you are overwhelmed and really need it.

Don't hesitate, though, to request it if you are not confident that you know where you are on the field. The last thing you want to do is wander aimlessly on the ground at an unfamiliar airport.

Runway Heading

Magnetic heading of the runway. If the runway is 10 but the magnetic heading of the runway is 104 degrees, the "runway heading" is 104, not 100. Pilots will often be told to fly runway heading after a takeoff.

Stop and Go

A stop and go is a landing where after touching down, the aircraft is brought to a complete stop, then a takeoff is performed from the spot in which the aircraft initially came to a stop.

Navigation

Abeam

If you are "abeam" something, it means the object is 90 degrees to the left or right of the track of your aircraft.

The most common example is "abeam the touchdown point," which describes your position on the downwind leg of a traffic pattern when the runway touchdown point is 90 degrees off of your flight path. This is often the point at which you start, or continue, to configure the aircraft for landing.

Direct

Instruction to fly a straight path to a navigation aid, fix, or point. This is usually used in IFR operations while receiving radar vectors, but it's not exclusive to IFR. If instructed by ATC to fly direct to a certain location, this would require you to deviate from the current route.

ETA

Estimated time of arrival. Can be calculated by taking the ETE and adding it to the time of departure. ATC will ask for this on occasion, especially on a cross-country flight.

Communications

ETE

The total time it will take from departure to landing (takeoff to touchdown). This is a term commonly used in cross-country flights. Sometimes ATC will ask for it.

TFR

Short for "temporary flight restriction." Always know where the TFRs are when flying, unless you want an F-16 off your wing.

ATC Radar Services

CONVECTIVE SIGMET

A **SIGMET** is "Significant Meteorological Information."

A **CONVECTIVE SIGMET** is related to convective activity (thunderstorms).

Pay close attention if you are on a cross-country flight and ATC comes on the radio discussing a **Convective Sigmet**.

All SIGMETs as well as all Airmen's Meteorological Information (AIRMET) are important; however, a Convective Sigmet can often pop up unexpectedly. This is all the more reason to conduct ample study of the weather before every flight away from your home base.

Flight Following and Traffic Advisories

As a VFR pilot, you may request "flight following" or "traffic advisories" from ATC when you would like to be informed of other traffic in your proximity. This commonly-used procedure is utilized to help you safely avoid other aircraft. You may request flight following at any point during your flight as long as you are in the radar range of the facility you are contacting.

An example traffic advisory from ATC could be "Cessna 3383T, traffic two o'clock, three miles, eastbound, six-thousand." This advisory tells you to start looking out of your right side for an aircraft at six-thousand feet. Once you make visual contact with the traffic, you can respond with "Traffic in Sight" or "Negative Contact" if you don't see the traffic.

Important: The PIC is ultimately responsible for avoiding aircraft on a VFR flight. VFR advisories are issued from ATC on a workload permitting basis. IFR traffic is a higher priority than VFR, so you are not guaranteed to get an advisory issued to you when controller workload is high.

IDENT

When controllers tells a pilot to "ident" they are asking them to press a button on the transponder that allows them to see where you are on radar. It helps with aircraft identification and allows the controller to confirm they are seeing the correct aircraft.

Negative Contact

If you are issued a traffic advisory, and after visually searching for the traffic, you still don't see them, you can inform ATC "negative contact on the traffic." This will let them know you can't see the traffic and may need further assistance locating them. Usually, they will continue to update you if a potential collision is imminent, but traffic avoidance under VFR is the PIC's responsibility.

Numerous Targets in Vicinity

This is a term used to let pilots know that there are numerous aircraft in a location in which they have requested advisories. This is used in lieu of individual traffic advisories for each aircraft that poses a hazard.

Radar Contact

This is the term ATC will use to let you know they see you on their radar and have positively identified you. The most common times you will hear this is when you have requested "flight following" and are contacting a departure controller, and when arriving at an airport and requesting traffic advisories on your way in.

Communications

Radar Contact Lost

ATC is no longer painting (viewing) you on their radar.

Radar Services Terminated

This term is used by ATC to let you know they are no longer providing traffic advisory services that have been previously been provided.

Resume Own Navigation

This term is used mostly while on an IFR flight plan; but after receiving radar vectors (heading/s) assigned to you), ATC will tell you when to resume navigating independently of their instructions by using this phrase.

Squawk VFR

"Squawk" means to dial your transponder to a specific code. "VFR" means transponder code 1200. This is the code that VFR aircraft are advised to use, unless otherwise instructed by an ATC facility.

Traffic in Sight

If issued a traffic advisory, this is the phrase used to inform ATC that you have spotted the aircraft.

Traffic No Factor

If a traffic advisory has been issued to you by ATC and is determined to be "no factor," it means that it no longer poses a safety hazard and separation is adequate.

Traffic No Longer Observed

This means that the controller can no longer see targets (aircraft) on his/her radar that were previously issued in an advisory. It DOES NOT, however, assure that there are no aircraft. It simply means the controller can't see them on the radar scope.

Many times, when you inform a controller that you are switching radio frequencies to a Common Traffic Advisory Frequency (CTAF) for an

LEARNING TO FLY - ESSENTIAL ELEMENTS

uncontrolled airport, they will tell you, "no traffic observed in the pattern," to help you familiarize yourself with what they see. On the other hand, they will often say "numerous targets observed in the vicinity of XYZ airport."

The Aeronautical Information Manual (AIM) is another essential resource for pilots and student pilots. It can be found online at www.faa.gov/air_traffic/publications/atpubs/aim_html/index.html.

Chapter 20
Common Abbreviations, Symbols, and Acronyms

> It is vital that pilots know and understand this "Aviation Vocabulary." These memory devices aid in ensuring safe operations and allow pilots to quickly communicate information.

Of course, committing these Acronyms, Abbreviations, and Symbols to memory will not happen overnight. It takes time, so slow and steady wins the race: consistent, gradual progress is most effective. Again, flash cards are very beneficial in speeding up the learning process. You *can* eat an elephant one bite at a time!

20.1 Abbreviations and Symbols

AFM: aircraft flight manual

AGL: above ground level

ALS: approach light systems

APU: auxiliary power unit

ASR: airport surveillance radar

LEARNING TO FLY - ESSENTIAL ELEMENTS

ATC: air traffic control

ATS: air traffic service

CAMP: continuous airworthiness maintenance program

CAS: calibrated airspeed

CAT II: Category II

CMP: configuration, maintenance, and procedures

DH: decision height

DME: distance measuring equipment compatible with TACAN

EAS: equivalent airspeed

EFVS: enhanced flight vision system

Equal Time Point: a point on the route of flight where the flight time, considering wind, to each of two selected airports is equal

ETOPS: extended operations

EWIS: electrical wiring interconnection system

FAA: Federal Aviation Administration

FFS: full flight simulator

FM: fan marker

FSTD: flight simulation training device

FTD: flight training device

GS: glide slope

HIRL: high-intensity runway light system

IAS: indicated airspeed

ICAO: International Civil Aviation Organization

IFR: instrument flight rules

Common Abbreviations, Symbols, and Acronyms

IFSD: in-flight shutdown

ILS: instrument landing system

IM: ILS inner marker

INT: intersection

LDA: localizer-type directional aid

LFR: low-frequency radio range

LMM: compass locator at middle marker

LOC: ILS localizer

LOM: compass locator at outer marker

M: mach number

MAA: maximum authorized IFR altitude

MALS: medium intensity approach light system

MALSR: medium intensity approach light system with runway alignment indicator lights

MCA: minimum crossing altitude

MDA: minimum descent altitude

MEA: minimum en route IFR altitude

MEL: minimum equipment list

MM: ILS middle marker

MOCA: minimum obstruction clearance altitude

MRA: minimum reception altitude

MSL: mean sea level

NDB (ADF): nondirectional beacon (automatic direction finder)

NM: nautical mile

LEARNING TO FLY - ESSENTIAL ELEMENTS

NOPAC: North Pacific area of operation

NOPT: no procedure turn required

OEI: one engine inoperative

OM: ILS outer marker

OPSPECS: operations specifications

PACOTS: Pacific Organized Track System

PAR: precision approach radar

PMA: parts manufacturer approval

POC: portable oxygen concentrator

PTRS: performance tracking and reporting system

RAIL: runway alignment indicator light system

RBN: radio beacon

RCLM: runway centerline marking

RCLS: runway centerline light system

REIL: runway end identification lights

RFFS: rescue and firefighting services

RNAV: area navigation

RR: low or medium frequency radio range station

RVR: runway visual range as measured in the touchdown zone area

SALS: short approach light system

SATCOM: satellite communications

SSALS: simplified short approach light system

SSALSR: simplified short approach light system with runway alignment indicator lights

Common Abbreviations, Symbols, and Acronyms

TACAN: ultra-high frequency tactical air navigational aid

TAS: true airspeed

TCAS: traffic alert and collision avoidance system

TDZL: touchdown zone lights

TSO: technical standard order

TVOR: very high frequency terminal omnirange station

V_A: design maneuvering speed

V_B: design speed for maximum gust intensity

V_C: design cruising speed

V_D: design diving speed

V_{DF}/M_{DF}: demonstrated flight diving speed

V_{EF}: the speed at which the critical engine is assumed to fail during takeoff

V_F: design flap speed

V_{FC}/M_{FC}: maximum speed for stability characteristics

V_{FE}: maximum flap extended speed

V_{FTO}: final takeoff speed

V_H: maximum speed in level flight with maximum continuous power

V_{LE}: maximum landing gear extended speed

V_{LO}: maximum landing gear operating speed

V_{LOF}: lift-off speed

V_{MC}: minimum control speed with the critical engine inoperative

V_{MO}/M_{MO}: maximum operating limit speed

V_{MU}: minimum unstick speed

LEARNING TO FLY - ESSENTIAL ELEMENTS

V_{NE}: never-exceed speed

V_{NO}: maximum structural cruising speed

V_R: rotation speed

V_{REF}: reference landing speed

V_S: the stalling speed or the minimum steady flight speed at which the aircraft is controllable

V_{S0}: the stalling speed or the minimum steady flight speed in the landing configuration

V_{S1}: the stalling speed or the minimum steady flight speed obtained in a specific configuration

V_{SR}: reference stall speed

V_{SR0}: reference stall speed in the landing configuration

V_{SR1}: reference stall speed in a specific configuration

V_{SW}: speed at which onset of natural or artificial stall warning occurs

V_{TOSS}: takeoff safety speed for Category A rotorcraft

V_X: speed for best angle of climb

V_Y: speed for best rate of climb

V_1: the maximum speed in the takeoff at which the pilot must take the first action (e.g., apply brakes, reduce thrust, deploy speed brakes) to stop the aircraft within the accelerate-stop distance

V_1: also the minimum speed in the takeoff, following a failure of the critical engine at V_{EF}, at which the pilot can continue the takeoff and achieve the required height above the takeoff surface within the takeoff distance

V_2: takeoff safety speed

V_{2min}: minimum takeoff safety speed

VFR: visual flight rules

Common Abbreviations, Symbols, and Acronyms

VGSI: visual glide slope indicator

VHF: very high frequency

VOR: very high frequency omnirange station

VORTAC: collocated VOR and TACAN

* * *

20.2 Acronyms for Procedure and Safety Checklists

The following sampling of acronyms assists and reminds pilots of important safety and procedure checks that must be completed before taking an aircraft into flight. Take advantage of what works for your purposes, whether flying commercial, corporate, or private.

AV1ATES (Airworthiness)
A - Annual Inspection
V - VOR Check (30 days)
1 - 100 Hour Inspection (if for hire)
A - Airworthiness Directives (ADs)
T - Transponder Check (24 months)
E - ELT (inspected every 12 months, battery replaced at half its lifespan or after one hour of use)
S - Static System Check (24 months)

NWKRAFT (Flight Planning)
N - NOTAMS
W - Weather
K - Known Air Traffic Control Delays
R - Runway Lengths
A - Alternate Airport
F - Fuel (enough to reach the destination, plus an alternate, and 45 minutes at cruising speed)
T - Takeoff and Landing Distances

LEARNING TO FLY - ESSENTIAL ELEMENTS

A TOMATO FLAMES (VFR Requirements)
A - Altimeter
T - Tachometer
O - Oil Pressure Gauge
M - Magnetic Compass
A - Airspeed Indicator
T - Temperature Gauge
O - Oil Temperature Gauge
F - Fuel Gauge
L - Landing Gear Indicator
A - Anti Collision Lights
M - Manifold Pressure Gauge
E - Emergency Equipment (emergency locator transmitter)
S - Seat Belts

—Ensures the **Minimum Equipment List (MEL)** is met: refers to the instruments, equipment, and procedures needed to perform the flight within the flight rules under which a pilot intends to fly.

FLAPS (VFR NIGHT)
F - Fuses
L - Landing Lights
A - Anti Collision Lights
P - Position Lights
S - Source of Power

GRAB CARD D (IFR Requirements)
G - Generator or Alternator
R - Radio (comms/nav) Appropriate to the Flight
A - Attitude Indicator
B - Ball (inclinometer)
C - Clock
A - Altimeter (pressure-sensitive)
R - Rate of Turn Indicator
D - Directional Gyro
D- DME or RNAV (flights above FL240)

Common Abbreviations, Symbols, and Acronyms

GRABCARDD is an IFR checklist of the minimum equipment required to be onboard the aircraft when operating a flight on instruments.

MARVELOUS VFR C500 (Mandatory IFR Reports)
M - Missed Approach
A - Airspeed Changes More Than 10 Knots or Five Percent
R - Reaching a Holding Fix
V - VFR-On-Top Altitude Changes
E - ETA Change More Than Three Minutes (no radar)
L - Leaving a Holding Fix
O - Outer Marker Inbound (no radar)
U - Unforecasted Weather
S - Safety of Flight Issues
V - Vacating an Altitude
F - Final Approach Fix Inbound (no radar)
R - Radio or Nav Failures
C - Compulsory Reporting Points (no radar)
500 FPM Climb or Descent Unable

—This acronym stands for a particular kind of report pilots must make to ATC or Flight Service Station (FSS) without being asked.

—A pilot who fails to report any of these may lead to grave penalties, including revoking your pilot's certificate or worse: an aircraft collision.

LOST COMMS - IFR

(For Altitude)
M - Minimum Charted (altitude for the area)
E - Expected (altitude)
A - Assigned (altitude)

(For Route)
A - Assigned (route)
V - Vectored (route)
E - Expected (route)
F - Filed (route as filed)

LEARNING TO FLY - ESSENTIAL ELEMENTS

COMPASS ERRORS

(Acceleration Errors)
A - Accelerate
N - North
D - Decelerate
S - South

(Dip Errors)
U - Undershoot
N - North
O - Overshoot
S - South

ANC

A - Aviate
N - Navigate
C - Communicate

Chapter 21
Advanced Qualification Program (AQP)

> The Advanced Qualification Program (AQP) is a voluntary alternative for pilot "training and checking" to the traditional regulatory requirements under CFR 14, Parts 121 (airlines) and 135 (charter).

The Airlines and most Charter Operators have their own training departments. Under AQP, they design and implement data collected from all operations, create scenarios from this data, and implement procedures in pilot training to validate proficiency strategies.

This training concept provides a **"Response Component"** to changes in aircraft technology, operations, and training methodologies as well as an increase in aviation safety. This alternate training concept replaces traditional requirements in flight checks, such as items normally checked by an examiner on a Practical Flight Test.

The result is a multi-faceted CRM approach to all aspects of flight safety designed to keep pilots alive and accident rates down. The Airlines and Charter Operations enjoy a far greater safety level as compared to GA. The AQP program validates their level of safety.

LEARNING TO FLY - ESSENTIAL ELEMENTS

As a GA student progresses through the private pilot syllabus, the ultimate goal is to meet the standards of the ACS guide to pass and receive a pilot certificate. Although SBT is addressed here, emphasis is placed on correctly demonstrating each required maneuver the applicant is asked to complete.

Once the student earns a Private Pilot Certificate and begins real-world flying experiences, **Flight Reviews** become the proficiency template. To date, AQP has not been considered by the FAA in regard to GA. However, there is currently a movement in this country to incorporate custom-designed GA flight reviews to target specific GA aviation accident causes that have a direct connection with real-world scenarios. **Spearheaded by Josh Flowers at Aviation101,** this approach to safety pinpoints exactly what may be needed to avoid such accidents.

Is it Legal?

Flight Review Requirements in FAA Advisory Circular AC 61-98E (4.1.1) specify only "a review of those maneuvers and procedures that, at the discretion of the person giving the review, are necessary for the pilot to demonstrate the safe exercise of the privileges of the pilot certificate." So there is leeway to custom-build a training program unique to *your* aircraft and type of flying.

FAA Advisory Circular AC 61-98E (1.9.1) Currency Criteria encourages this custom design: "Pilots should design a currency program tailored to their individual operating environments and needs, which should emphasize proficiency beyond the minimum currency requirements."

I would encourage pilots and flight instructors to consider tailoring their flying and flight reviews with these AQP concepts. Part 121 and Part 135 operators use it. It works! The objective is to reduce the accident rate, and this program would be a great addition to GA.

Download a complete copy of the AQP Annual Flight Review (AFR) Guidelines at Aviation101.com/aqpgrassroots.

Advanced Qualification Program (AQP)

The following pages include a few helpful excerpts from the AQP AFR Supplemental Document provided by Josh Flowers at Aviation 101.

General Aviation AQP AFR Flight Profile (Sample)

A breakdown of each topic may be found in the supplementary document at Aviation101.com/aqpgrassroots.

- ___ Pre-flight Preparation
- ___ **ADM**
- ___ Before Taxi Check
- ___ Preflight Briefing
- ___ Rejected Takeoff
- ___ Intentional-**IMC** or Unintentional-IMC **ATO**
- ___ **LOTOT** (either single or twin)
- ___ **SD**-D or SD-N (day or night)
- ___ Terrain Avoidance
- ___ Loss of **AHRS** in Flight
- ___ Autopilot Failure
- ___ Loss of Speed Awareness
- ___ Mishandled Abnormal in Flight
- ___ Stabilized Approach
- ___ Messed up Go-Arounds
- ___ Importance of the Flight Review

ADM: Aeronautical Decision Making
AHRS: Attitude and Heading Referencing System
ATO: After Takeoff
IMC: Instrument Meteorological Conditions
LOTOT: Loss of Thrust on Takeoff
SD: Spatial Disorientation

As a CFI, it's important to know your students/pilots. Pilots are different, so not every AQP AFR will address all items in the above profile. **Customize it!** This is easily done by having a casual conversation with the student/pilot receiving the Flight Review: "How long have you been flying?" "What type of flying do you normally do?" "ASEL, AMEL, IFR, VFR, Day, Night?"

The idea here is to get to know who is sitting across from you in an effort to help *them*, so asking meaningful questions in a casual manner will immensely help when stepping through the relevant tasks during the ground portion of the review.

LOSS OF CONTROL (LOC-I)

It's not the fall that will kill you - it's that sudden STOP at the end. **Loss-of-Control (LOC)** has become all too common on the stage of GA accidents. Blunt trauma is almost always the cause of death in a fatal aircraft accident.

Loss of Control Inflight (LOC-I) may be presented in two frameworks:

1. Uncontrolled Flight Into Terrain (U-FIT), commonly referred to as **Loss of Control In-Flight) (LOC-I).** In this scenario, the aircraft is not responsive to flight control inputs due to lack of airflow over the wings (stall/spin event), a pilot's incapacitation preventing any pilot control, or a mechanical malfunction.

2. Controlled Flight Into Terrain (C-FIT). In this scenario, the aircraft is responsive to flight control inputs until impact and may involve one of these examples**:**

- Spatial Disorientation (SD), day (D) or night (N)
- Intentional Instrument Meteorological Conditions (I-IMC) after takeoff (ATO): i.e., a departing IFR flight
- An Unintentional IMC (U-IMC) ATO (a surprised VFR pilot rotating up into the clouds)
- A Minimum Controllable Airspeed (VMC) roll over Loss of Control Inflight (LOC-I) due to an inoperative engine inflight with a twin engine aircraft
- A Loss Of Thrust On Takeoff (LOTOT) due to an engine failure

Advanced Qualification Program (AQP)

The following list of GA Fatal Accidents with Possible Scenarios and Solutions is a convenient tool for the flight instructor to evaluate the pilot under review. You will notice that every possible scenario lists a solution.

AVIATION 101
www.aviation101.com

GENERAL AVIATION FATAL ACCIDENTS: POSSIBLE SCENARIOS

CONTROLS STILL WORKING AT IMPACT (C-FIT)

- ☐ 1. SD-D
  solution: Foggles* + Proficiency
- ☐ 2. SD-N
  solution: Foggles* + Proficiency
- ☐ 3. I-IMC ATO
  solution: Proficiency
- ☐ 4. U-IMC ATO
  solution: Foggles* + Proficiency
- ☐ 5. BUZZING/ACRO
  solution: Avoid
- ☐ 6. MISHANDLED ABN
  solution: Proficiency
- ☐ 7. TERRAIN COLLISION
  solution: ForeFlight (iPad, tablet)
- ☐ 8. LOSS OF AHRS IN FLT
  solution: ForeFlight (iPad, tablet)
- ☐ 9. NON-STABILIZED APPCH
  solution: Proficiency
- ☐ 10. intentionally left blank

CONTROLS NOT WORKING AT IMPACT (U-FIT)

- ☐ 11. LOTOT
  solution: Proficiency
- ☐ 12. LOSS OF SPEED AWARENESS
  solution: DMMS + Proficiency
- ☐ 13. VMC ROLL OVER
  solution: Proficiency
- ☐ 14. MID-AIR COLLISION
  solution: ADS-B + ForeFlight
- ☐ 15. IN FLIGHT ICING
  solution: Avoid
- ☐ 16. MESSED UP GO-AROUND
  solution: Proficiency
- ☐ 17. FAILED FLT CONTROL SYSTEM
  solution: Preflight/Maintenance
- ☐ 18. REJECTED TAKEOFF (RTO)
  solution: Proficiency
- ☐ 19. SEAT SLIDES BACK
  solution: Preflight/Maintenance
- ☐ 20. intentionally left blank

These solutions are explained at length in the supplemental document at Aviation101.com/aqpgrassroots.

LEARNING TO FLY - ESSENTIAL ELEMENTS

Being aware of the problem and practicing and reviewing in advance will cause drastic improvement in the outcome.

You may practice with FOGGLES™ (glasses designed to limit the pilot's field of vision) on a lanyard around your neck; having them at the ready for quick donning may mitigate the Startle Effect and force you to focus on the attitude gyro and instruments.

The General Aviation Accident Dashboard

The National Transportation Safety Board (NTSB) has released an online tool displaying information on GA accidents, investigation findings, and safety recommendations. The GA Accident Dashboard allows users to filter information by year, location, flight phase, and defining event.

The dashboard and tutorials may be found at https://www.ntsb.gov/safety/data/Pages/GeneralAviationDashboard.aspx.

Chapter 22
Recommended Reading

I enjoy reading and learning about anything related to aviation. The following booklist contains a few favorites in my aviation library. Although this is not a comprehensive list, the professional pilot should be familiar with most, if not all, of these superb books.

Buck, R. (2013). <u>Weather Flying</u> (5th ed.). New York, London: McGraw-Hill.

Durden, R. (2012). <u>The Thinking Pilot's Flight Manual</u> (Vol. 1): Renaissance Aviation.

FAA Staff. (2021). <u>Airplane Flying Handbook (FAA-H-8083-3C)</u>. OK: USDOT.

FAA Staff. (2016). <u>Pilot's Handbook of Aeronautical Knowledge (FAA-H-8083-25B)</u>. OK: USDOT.

FAA Staff. (2021). <u>Instrument Procedures Handbook (FAA-H-8083-16B). OK: USDOT</u>.

Gann, E. (1986). <u>Fate is the Hunter</u>. New York: Simon & Schuster.

Kershner, W.K. (2017). <u>The Student Pilot's Flight Manual</u> (11th ed.). Newcastle, WA: ASA, Inc.

Kershner, W.K. (2018). <u>The Flight Instructor's Manual</u> (6th ed.). Newcastle, WA: ASA, Inc.

Langewiesche, Wolfgang. (1990). <u>Stick and Rudder</u>. New York, London: McGraw-Hill.

Langewiesche, William. (1999). <u>Inside the Sky</u>. New York, London: Knopf Doubleday.

Lindbergh, C.A. (2003). <u>The Spirit of St. Louis</u>. New York: Scribner.

Machado, R. (2020). <u>Rod Machado's How to Fly an Airplane Handbook</u>. San Clemente, CA: The Aviation Speakers Bureau.

Machado, R. (2021). <u>Rod Machado's Private Pilot Handbook</u> (3rd ed.). San Clemente, CA: The Aviation Speakers Bureau.

McCullough, D. (2016). <u>The Wright Brothers</u>. New York: Simon & Schuster.

Paine Jr, Lauran. (2009). <u>The Flying Life</u>. Pasadena, CA: Cascade.

Saint-Exupéry, A. (1974). <u>Night Flight</u>. Boston, New York: HarperCollins.

Saint-Exupéry, A. (1967). <u>Wind, Sand, and Stars</u>. Boston, New York: HarperCollins.

Schappert, J. (2022). <u>Private Pilot Blueprint</u>. Orlando, FL: Gulfstream Media LLC.

Schiff, B. (1997). <u>The Proficient Pilot</u> (Vol. 1). Newcastle, WA: ASA, Inc.

Schiff, B. (2001). <u>The Proficient Pilot</u> (Vol 2). Newcastle, WA: ASA, Inc.

Schiff, B. (1997). <u>Flying Wisdom, The Proficient Pilot</u> (Vol. 3). Newcastle, WA: ASA, Inc.

Appendix: Aviation Terminology and Abbreviations

List of Abbreviations used in this Text

ACR: Airman Certification Representative
ACS: Airman Certification Standards
ADI: Attitude Director Indicator
ADM: Aeronautical Decision Making
AFM: Aircraft Flight Manual
AFR: Annual Flight Review
AGL: Above Ground Level
AHRS: Attitude and Heading Referencing System
AIM: Aeronautical Information Manual
AME: Aviation Medical Examiner
AMEL: Airplane Multi-Engine Land
AOA: Angle of Attack
AQP: Advanced Qualification Program
ASEL: Airplane Single-Engine Land
ATC: Air Traffic Control
ATO: After Takeoff
ATP: Airline Transport Pilot
BI: Basic Instruments
C-AOA: Critical Angle of Attack
CFI: Certified Flight Instructor
CFII: Certified Flight Instructor Instrument
C-FIT: Controlled Flight into Terrain
CFR: Code of Federal Regulations
CRM: Crew Resource Management
DG: Directional Gyro
DMMS: Defined Minimum Maneuver Speed
DPE: Designated Pilot Examiner
FAA: Federal Aviation Administration
FAF: Final Approach Fix
FAR: Federal Aviation Regulations
FSS: Flight Service Station
GA: General Aviation
HP: High Performance
IACRA: Integrated Airman Certification and Rating Application
ICAO: International Civil Aviation Organization

Appendix: Aviation Terminology and Abbreviations

IFR: Instrument Flight Rules
I-IMC: Intentional Instrument Meteorological Conditions
IMC: Instrument Meteorological Conditions
IVSI: Instantaneous Vertical Speed Indicator
KT: Knot (s)
LOC: Loss of Control
LOC-I: Loss of Control Inflight
LOTOT: Loss of Thrust on Takeoff
MP: Manifold Pressure
NAFI: National Association of Flight Instructors
NM: Nautical Mile
NOTAMS: Notice to Airmen
NTSB: National Transportation Safety Board
PIC: Pilot in Command
POH: Pilot Operating Handbook
RCAM: Runway Conditions Assessment Matrix
RPM: Revolutions Per Minute
RTO: Rejected Takeoff
SA: Situational Awareness
SBT: Scenario Based Training
SD: Spacial Disorientation
SRM: Single Pilot Resource Management
U-FIT: Uncontrolled Flight Into Terrain
U-IMC: Unintentional Instrument Meteorological Conditions
VFR: Visual Flight Rules
VMC: Visual Meteorological Conditions
VNAV: Vertical Navigation

About the Author

John Berkstresser has been instructing GA Pilots for almost 50 years. He was motivated to fly as early as he can remember while growing up next door to a grass airport strip, mesmerized by J-3 Piper Cubs flying all day long. His passion and focus have never waned.

A graduate of the United States Naval Flight Officer Program, John completed two sea tours in the F-4 Phantom followed by an instructor assignment in the A-4 Skyhawk training squadron in Kingsville, Texas. He began working in GA shortly after leaving the Navy.

John earned his Gold Seal Flight Instructor Certificate while teaching preparatory high school students at the Harlingen, Texas, Marine Military Academy and while flight instructing at McAllen Aviation in McAllen, Texas. His ratings include ATP, CFI, CFII, MEI, and SES.

He has amassed over 5,000 hours in most GA aircraft and over 27,000 hours in jet aircraft. He has attended 16 jet schools and has 12 jet type ratings. John retired after 32 years with the airlines and five years subsequently with a jet charter service.

John continues teaching young people to prepare for careers in aviation, whether it be military or civilian. He is based at Martin Campbell Field Airport in Copperhill, Tennessee.

He resides in the Blue Ridge Mountains of Ellijay, Georgia, with his wife, Lynne, and their dog, Penny.

Made in the USA
Columbia, SC
16 June 2025